English Lessons Through Literature

Aspiring

Kathy Jo DeVore

www.barefootmeandering.com

veritas • gnaritas • libertas

ad majorem Dei gloriam

et liberis meis

Table of Contents

Introduction

A total of eight levels of *English Lessons Through Literature* have been planned which will take children through elementary and middle school grammar and composition. Lessons also include literature and poetry, handwriting through copywork, and spelling through prepared dictation, making it a complete language arts program.

Each level of this program has three lessons per week for thirty-six weeks—a total of 108 lessons per year. Each lesson includes a literature selection, a poem, and either a short story or a picture study. In Levels A and B, the stories are all Aesop's fables.

Level A is intended for a first or second grade child who is ready for copywork and is beginning to read fluently; the student should at least be able to sound out the copywork. Completion of Level A is not a prerequisite for Level B. Level B is intended for a second or third grade child—or for older children in need of remediation. In our own household, we prefer to delay formal education a bit, so my children begin ELTL in second grade with Level A.

Level A is an intentionally light program. The focus of Level A is to begin teaching usage and mechanics of the English language through copywork. Although Level A has written lessons for many (but not all) of the lessons, the real lessons are the copywork selections. It is while practicing copywork that children will learn and internalize proper spelling, capitalization, and punctuation while practicing handwriting. The lessons in Level A merely point out and reinforce concepts to children before they begin copywork. Children are introduced to punctuation marks, quotations, and contractions. They then practice writing them.

In Level B, children are introduced to the parts of speech as well as lists of helping verbs, prepositions, etc. Examples and exercises consist of a passage from the literature or from a poem. In the exercises, children take what they have learned from the lesson and demonstrate understanding. The repetition necessary for mastery comes from constant review in the exercises rather than from long exercises. And by "mastery," I do not mean that children should have attained perfect understanding of the parts of speech by the end of Level B. Rather, children should be able to define each part of speech and find examples in real sentences. They will obtain further and more advanced practice in later levels.

I have occasionally simplified or modified sentences to avoid confusion, but I have tried to keep this to a minimum. Particularly in Level A, some sentences have been shortened to make them a more appropriate length for copywork. Spelling and punctuation have been modified as necessary.

Literature Selections

The literature suggested in this book is in the public domain in the United States, and the full text of each story and book can be found online. Most are also available as audio books. A complete reading list appears at the beginning of each level.

Since most of the examples and part of the daily copywork come directly from the literature, reading the literature is an important component of this program. However, there is certainly room to skip books that the child does not like. Fairy tales may be disturbing to some children, and it is up to the parents to determine whether or not a recommended resource is right for their family. My homeschooling motto has long been, "Use the curriculum; don't let the curriculum use you." I recommend the motto more highly than I recommend any of the literature selections in this book.

I do recommend reading the literature prior to the lesson. The examples and the copywork almost always come from the reading selection from that day.

Copywork

This book contains a great deal of copywork. From the middle of Level A through Level B, most weeks have five pages of copywork consisting of one to four lines per page for each week: three pages from the literature selection, two with maxims, and one from the poetry selection. This amount of copywork would have made my oldest son cry. My second son wanted more copywork than this. If you find this is too much copywork for your child, there are several options:

1. Skip part of the copywork. Decide which portions of the copywork are most important to your goals, and have your child do only those.

2. If you'd rather have your child do all of the copywork, have the child do the copywork portions five days a week instead of three. This would be one page of copywork per day.

3. Have your child do copywork in the morning and again in the afternoon. If your child is doing copywork three days a week, this would be one page in the morning and one page in the afternoon twice a week with only one page of copywork on the last lesson day of the week. If your child is doing copywork five days per week, this would only be half a page at each sitting.

Narrations

Narrations occur every two weeks throughout all levels. Once the child is comfortable with narrating, you can include narration exercises from history and science reading as well. Levels A and B each include ninety Aesop's fables that could also be used for additional narration practice if desired.

Level A begins with picture narrations. After hearing a fable, children are asked to draw a picture of the story and tell about the picture. During the second half of the year, they will begin standard narrations.

The standard narrations at the end of Level A and throughout Level B start with the shortest Aesop's fables and gradually increase in length. The procedure for doing the narrations is quite simple: After hearing the fable, children tell the story back to their instructors in their own words while the instructors write the story down for the children. Remember that children are learning a brand new skill and may not understand exactly what is expected of them. Prompting them with questions helps. Ask questions such as, "What happened first?" and, "Then what happened?" Help them get the details of the story in the proper order. Since the instructor is doing the writing for the child, the child has no need to worry about spelling or punctuation. At this stage, I correct nothing more than grammatical errors—the sort that I would correct during normal conversation—and, occasionally, a detail from the story. These are best done at the end of the narration to avoid interrupting the child's train of thought. In Level B, part of the narration should be printed or written for the child to use as copywork for that day.

Approached this way, narrations follow a logical progression. Narrations first start with something many children are already doing: drawing pictures and telling about them. Next children begin telling about the story without the picture, though they may certainly draw a picture to illustrate the narration. Then, they begin copying their own words. Finally, they will begin writing the story down themselves without orally narrating it first. This final stage is not covered in this book.

Memory Work

Both levels include lists to memorize, and Level B includes many definitions to memorize as well. In Level A, the lists to learn are included in the lessons with instructions for memorization, and reviews are included in the lessons as well. However, poetry is not included in the lessons for memorization.

In Level B, grammatical concepts and lists are introduced in the lessons, but they should be memorized separately. Grammar memory work is included in Appendix A for quick and easy review.

I recommend a memory card system for poetry. I do not specify which poems to memorize. My suggestion is to begin memorizing the first poem of the level. When that is memorized, choose one of the poems that the child particularly liked from the preceding lessons, or one that you feel is particularly important, and begin memorizing it. Continue in this fashion throughout the year. There are 108 poems in each level, giving everyone a good selection from which to choose.

We use 5 x 8 index cards because there are binders available to hold them, but smaller index cards work just as well. Create dividers for three sections: Current, Short Term Review, and Long Term Review. One side of the card should have the title of the card (i.e. Definition of a Noun, Clouds by Christina G. Rossetti, etc.). The reverse has the memory selection.

Cards in the Current section should be read three times a day until the passage or definition has been memorized. The card can then move to the Short Term Review section, and that section can be reviewed once a week. Once the child has successfully recited a card several weeks in a row, it can go into the Long Term Review section for review once a month. You can also color code the cards by subject or topic.

Picture Study

All pictures of paintings in this book are, of necessity, black and white. I highly recommend searching online for color copies of the art to view online or print for studying. Color copies of the paintings are available as free downloads from my Lulu store for your convenience. Very light black and white copies of the artwork are included as coloring pages.

Optional Workbook

The suggested exercises and copywork are included in this book, so the workbook is truly optional. The benefits of purchasing the workbook are:

1. The PDF version of the workbook is a file that may be printed out for all the children in your family. It may not be resold.

2. The copywork is already typed in a handwriting font so that you don't have to type or write it for the child to copy. There are several popular handwriting styles from which to choose, and you get them all because you shouldn't have to buy a new workbook if you change handwriting styles with the next child.

Level
A

Level A: Aspiring Literature List

All the literature selections suggested herein are in the public domain in the United States of America and are probably available at your local library. The complete texts can also be found online from Project Gutenberg (www.gutenberg.org) and/or the Baldwin Project (www.mainlesson.com). Most are available as audio books, and free audio book versions may be found online from LibriVox (www.librivox.org).

This list shows in which lesson each book begins in parentheses after the book title.

Beatrix Potter Stories (Lesson 1)
    The twenty Beatrix Potter stories do not follow the order of any particular published edition of her work.

Just So Stories by Rudyard Kipling (Lesson 21)
    One of the stories, "How the Leopard Got His Spots," contains a racial slur near the end. Many newer versions of these stories have removed or changed this line.

Five Children and It by Edith Nesbit (Lesson 33)

The Jungle Book by Rudyard Kipling (Lesson 44)

Pinocchio by C. Collodi (Lesson 58)

The Orange Fairy Book by Andrew Lang, 10 stories (Lesson 76, Lesson 101)

The Velveteen Rabbit by Margery Williams (Lesson 83)

The Box-Car Children by Gertrude Chandler Warner (Lesson 84)

The King of the Golden River by John Ruskin (Lesson 104)

All the fables in Level A are from *The Aesop for Children* by Milo Winter.

1. Introducing Sentence Mechanics

• The Tale of Peter Rabbit by Beatrix Potter

Let's look at the first sentence from "The Tale of Peter Rabbit":

Once upon a time there were four little Rabbits.

Do you notice something different about the first word in the sentence? It starts with a capital letter! A sentence always starts with a capital letter, and it ends with a punctuation mark. There are three punctuation marks used to end sentences, and the most common one is the period. It's the little dot that you see at the end of a sentence.

Today you will begin copywork. That means you will copy a sentence from today's story, "The Tale of Peter Rabbit." When you copy your sentence, be sure to start it with a capital letter and end it with a period.

Happy Thought
By Robert Louis Stevenson

The world is so full of a number of things,
I'm sure we should all be as happy as kings.

The Wolf and the Kid
An Aesop's Fable

There was once a little Kid whose growing horns made him think he was a grown-up Billy Goat and able to take care of himself. So one evening when the flock started home from the pasture and his mother called, the Kid paid no heed and kept right on nibbling the tender grass. A little later when he lifted his head, the flock was gone.

He was all alone. The sun was sinking. Long shadows came creeping over the ground. A chilly little wind came creeping with them making scary noises in the grass. The Kid shivered as he thought of the terrible Wolf. Then he started wildly over the field, bleating for his mother. But not half-way, near a clump of trees, there was the Wolf!

The Kid knew there was little hope for him.

"Please, Mr. Wolf," he said trembling, "I know you are going to eat me. But first please pipe me a tune, for I want to dance and be merry as long as I can."

The Wolf liked the idea of a little music before eating, so he struck up a merry tune, and the Kid leaped and frisked gaily.

Meanwhile, the flock was moving slowly homeward. In the still evening air, the Wolf's piping carried far. The Shepherd Dogs pricked up their ears. They recognized the song the Wolf sings before a feast, and in a moment, they were racing back to the pasture. The Wolf's song ended suddenly, and as he ran, with the Dogs at his heels, he called himself a fool for turning piper to please a Kid when he should have stuck to his butcher's trade.

Do not let anything turn you from your purpose.

Copywork

Literature

Peter sat down to rest.

2. Sentence Mechanics

• The Tale of Squirrel Nutkin by Beatrix Potter

When you do your copywork today, remember to begin your sentence with a capital letter. Do you remember what the little dot at the end of the sentence is called? It's a punctuation mark, and it's called a period.

What is Pink?

By Christina G. Rossetti

What is pink? A rose is pink
By the fountain's brink.
What is red? A poppy's red
In its barley bed.
What is blue? The sky is blue
Where the clouds float through.
What is white? A swan is white
Sailing in the light.
What is yellow? Pears are yellow,
Rich and ripe and mellow.
What is green? The grass is green,
With small flowers between.
What is violet? Clouds are violet
In the summer twilight.
What is orange? Why, an orange,
Just an orange!

The Tortoise and the Ducks

An Aesop's Fable

The Tortoise, you know, carries his house on his back. No matter how hard he tries, he cannot leave home. They say that Jupiter punished him so because he was such a lazy stay-at-home that he would not go to Jupiter's wedding, even when especially invited.

After many years, Tortoise began to wish he had gone to that wedding. When he saw how gaily the birds flew about and how the Hare and the Chipmunk and all the other animals ran nimbly by, always eager to see everything there was to be seen, the Tortoise felt very sad and discontented. He wanted to see the world, too, and there he was with a house on his back and little short legs that could hardly drag him along.

One day he met a pair of Ducks and told them all his trouble.

"We can help you to see the world," said the Ducks. "Take hold of this stick with your teeth, and we will carry you far up in the air where you can see the whole countryside. But keep quiet or you will be sorry."

The Tortoise was very glad indeed. He seized the stick firmly with his teeth; the two Ducks took hold of it one at each end, and away they sailed up toward the clouds.

Just then a Crow flew by. He was very much astonished at the strange sight and cried, "This must surely be the King of Tortoises!"

"Why certainly——" began the Tortoise.

But as he opened his mouth to say these foolish words, he lost his hold on the stick, and down he fell to the ground where he was dashed to pieces on a rock.

Foolish curiosity and vanity often lead to misfortune.

Copywork

Literature

Now this riddle is as old as the hills.

Apple-Picking by Camille Pissarro

Picture Study

1. Read the title and the name of the artist. Study the picture for several minutes, then put the picture away.

2. Describe the picture.

3. Look at the picture again. Do you notice any details that you missed before? What do you like or dislike about this painting? Does it remind you of anything?

3. Sentence Mechanics; Picture Study: Apple-Picking

- The Tailor of Gloucester by Beatrix Potter

What kind of letter do we use to begin a sentence? What punctuation mark have we been using so far to end a sentence?

Did you remember? A sentence begins with a capital letter, and you've been ending sentences with period. Look at today's copywork sentence and point out the capital letter and the period:

The tailor worked and worked.

The Moon

By Robert Louis Stevenson

The moon has a face like the clock in the hall;
She shines on thieves on the garden wall,
On streets and fields and harbor quays,
And birdies asleep in the forks of the trees.

The squalling cat and the squeaking mouse,
The howling dog by the door of the house,
The bat that lies in bed at noon,
All love to be out by the light of the moon.

But all of the things that belong to the day
Cuddle to sleep to be out of her way;
And flowers and children close their eyes
Till up in the morning the sun shall arise.

Copywork

Literature

The tailor worked and worked.

4. Proper Names and Titles of Respect

- The Tale of Benjamin Bunny by Beatrix Potter

You've learned that we use a capital letter to begin a sentence. We also use capital letters when we write someone's name. Look at the names in these sentences from "The Tale of Benjamin Bunny":

> A gig was coming along the road. It was driven by <u>Mr. McGregor</u>, and beside him sat <u>Mrs. McGregor</u> in her best bonnet.

Mr. stands for **mister**, and it's a title of respect for a man. **Mrs.**, which we pronounce **missus**, stands for **mistress**, and it's a title of respect for a married lady. We use titles of respect to be polite. Since a title of respect is part of someone's name, we begin it with a capital letter. Notice that each title of respect also has a period at the end.

The Kind Moon

By Sara Teasdale

I think the moon is very kind
To take such trouble just for me.
He came along with me from home
To keep me company.

He went as fast as I could run;
I wonder how he crossed the sky?
I'm sure he hasn't legs and feet
Or any wings to fly.

Yet here he is above their roof;
Perhaps he thinks it isn't right
For me to go so far alone,
Though mother said I might.

The Dog, The Rooster, and the Fox

An Aesop's Fable

A Dog and a Rooster, who were the best of friends, wished very much to see something of the world. So they decided to leave the farmyard and to set out into the world along the road that led to the woods. The two comrades traveled along in the very best of spirits and without meeting any adventure to speak of.

At nightfall the Rooster, looking for a place to roost, as was his custom, spied nearby a hollow tree that he thought would do very nicely for a night's lodging. The Dog could creep inside, and the Rooster would fly up on one of the branches. So said, so done, and both slept very comfortably.

With the first glimmer of dawn, the Rooster awoke. For the moment he forgot just where he was. He thought he was still in the farmyard where it had been his duty to arouse the household at daybreak.

So standing on tip-toes, he flapped his wings and crowed lustily. But instead of awakening the farmer, he awakened a Fox not far off in the wood. The Fox immediately had rosy visions of a very delicious breakfast. Hurrying to the tree where the Rooster was roosting, he said very politely, "A hearty welcome to our woods, honored sir. I cannot tell you how glad I am to see you here. I am quite sure we shall become the closest of friends."

"I feel highly flattered, kind sir," replied the Rooster slyly. "If you will please go around to the door of my house at the foot of the tree, my porter will let you in."

The hungry but unsuspecting Fox went around the tree as he was told, and in a twinkling, the Dog had seized him.

Those who try to deceive may expect to be paid in their own coin.

Copywork

Literature

Old Mr. Bunny had no opinion whatever of cats.

5. Proper Names

- The Tale of Mrs. Tiggy-winkle by Beatrix Potter

Today your story was about Mrs. Tiggy-winkle and a little girl named Lucie. Do you remember what **Mrs.** means? It's a title of respect for a married lady. We capitalize it because it is part of someone's name, and we always begin names with a capital letter.

Do you know all of your names? Most people have three names: a first name, a middle name, and a last name. The last name is also called a family name because we share that name with members of our family. What are your first, middle, and last names?

Do you know what Mrs. Tiggy-winkle's husband's name would be?
Mr. Tiggy-winkle!

A Bird Came Down the Walk

By Emily Dickinson

A bird came down the walk:
He did not know I saw;
He bit an angle-worm in halves
And ate the fellow, raw.

And then he drank a dew
From a convenient grass,
And then hopped sidewise to the wall
To let a beetle pass.

He glanced with rapid eyes
That hurried all abroad,—
They looked like frightened beads, I thought;
He stirred his velvet head

Like one in danger; cautious,
I offered him a crumb,
And he unrolled his feathers
And rowed him softer home

Than oars divide the ocean,
Too silver for a seam,
Or butterflies, off banks of noon,
Leap, splashless, as they swim.

The Donkey and His Driver

An Aesop's Fable

A Donkey was being driven along a road leading down the mountain side when he suddenly took it into his silly head to choose his own path. He could see his stall at the foot of the mountain, and to him the quickest way down seemed to be over the edge of the nearest cliff. Just as he was about to leap over, his master caught him by the tail and tried to pull him back, but the stubborn Donkey would not yield and pulled with all his might.

"Very well," said his master, "go your way, you willful beast, and see where it leads you."

With that he let go, and the foolish Donkey tumbled head over heels down the mountain side.

They who will not listen to reason but stubbornly go their own way against the friendly advice of those who are wiser than they are on the road to misfortune.

Copywork

Literature

Then Mrs. Tiggy-winkle made tea.

6. Picture Narration: The Frogs and the Ox

- The Tale of Mr. Jeremy Fisher by Beatrix Potter

The Frogs and the Ox

An Aesop's Fable

An Ox came down to a reedy pool to drink. As he splashed heavily into the water, he crushed a young Frog into the mud. The old Frog soon missed the little one and asked his brothers and sisters what had become of him.

"A great big monster," said one of them, "stepped on little brother with one of his huge feet!"

"Big, was he!" said the old Frog, puffing herself up. "Was he as big as this?"

"Oh, much bigger!" they cried.

The Frog puffed up still more.

"He could not have been bigger than this," she said. But the little Frogs all declared that the monster was much, much bigger, and the old Frog kept puffing herself out more and more until, all at once, she burst.

Do not attempt the impossible.

Seal Lullaby

By Rudyard Kipling

Oh, hush thee, my baby, the night is behind us,
And black are the waters that sparkled so green,
The moon o'er the combers, looks downward to find us
At rest in the hollows that rustle between.
Where billow meets billow, there soft be thy pillow;
Ah, weary wee flipperling, curl at thy ease!
The storm shall not wake thee, nor shark overtake thee,
Asleep in the arms of the slow-swinging seas.

Copywork

But Mr. Jeremy liked getting his feet wet.

Picture Narration

Draw a picture of the Aesop's fable from today. Show your picture to your instructor and tell her about it.

7. Introducing Quotation Marks

• The Tale of Mr. Tod by Beatrix Potter

There are many different punctuation marks. Punctuation marks tell us things about what we are reading. So far, you've learned about the period. The period tells us that a sentence is ending.

Today we're going to talk about quotation marks. They look like this:

" "

Have you seen these before in your reading? Quotation marks tell us that someone is saying something. They show us when someone begins speaking in a story and when that person finishes speaking. Look at this quote from "The Tale of Mr. Tod." Point out the quotation marks.

> "I did think they were kicking rather hard for caterpillars."

The quotation marks wrap around the words that Peter Rabbit said.

Hurt No Living Thing

By Christina G. Rossetti

Hurt no living thing:
Ladybird, nor butterfly,
Nor moth with dusty wing,
Nor cricket chirping cheerily,
Nor grasshopper so light of leap,
Nor dancing gnat, nor beetle fat,
Nor harmless worms that creep.

The Oxen and the Wheels

An Aesop's Fable

A pair of Oxen were drawing a heavily loaded wagon along a miry country road. They had to use all their strength to pull the wagon, but they did not complain.

The Wheels of the wagon were of a different sort. Though the task they had to do was very light compared with that of the Oxen, they creaked and groaned at every turn. The poor Oxen, pulling with all their might to draw the wagon through the deep mud, had their ears filled with the loud complaining of the Wheels. And this, you may well know, made their work so much the harder to endure.

"Silence!" the Oxen cried at last, out of patience. "What have you Wheels to complain about so loudly? We are drawing all the weight, not you, and we are keeping still about it besides."

They complain most who suffer least.

Copywork

Literature

"He had a sack with something alive in it."

8. Quotations

• The Tale of Mrs. Tittlemouse by Beatrix Potter

We call the exact words that someone has spoken a **quote** or a **quotation**. That's why we call the punctuation marks that tell us someone is speaking **quotation marks**. They point out a quotation.

> "Good-day, Babbitty Bumble. I should be glad to buy some beeswax."

Point out the quotation marks in the sentence above from "The Tale of Mrs. Tittlemouse." Notice that the period comes before the ending quotation mark.

Robin Redbreast

By William Allingham

Good-bye, good-bye to Summer!
For Summer's nearly done;
The garden smiling faintly,
Cool breezes in the sun;
Our Thrushes now are silent,
Our Swallows flown away,—
But Robin's here, in coat of brown,
With ruddy breast-knot gay.
Robin, Robin Redbreast,
O Robin dear!
Robin singing sweetly
In the falling of the year.

Bright yellow, red, and orange,
The leaves come down in hosts;
The trees are Indian Princes,
But soon they'll turn to Ghosts;
The scanty pears and apples
Hang russet on the bough,

It's Autumn, Autumn, Autumn late,
'Twill soon be Winter now.
Robin, Robin Redbreast,
O Robin dear!
And welaway! my Robin,
For pinching times are near.

The fireside for the Cricket,
The wheatstack for the Mouse,
When trembling night-winds whistle
And moan all round the house;
The frosty ways like iron,
The branches plumed with snow,—
Alas! in Winter, dead and dark,
Where can poor Robin go?
Robin, Robin Redbreast,
O Robin dear!
And a crumb of bread for Robin,
His little heart to cheer.

The Goatherd and the Wild Goats

An Aesop's Fable

One cold, stormy day, a Goatherd drove his Goats for shelter into a cave where a number of Wild Goats had also found their way. The Shepherd wanted to make the Wild Goats part of his flock, so he fed them well. But to his own flock, he gave only just enough food to keep them alive. When the weather cleared and the Shepherd led the Goats out to feed, the Wild Goats scampered off to the hills.

"Is that the thanks I get for feeding you and treating you so well?" complained the Shepherd.

"Do not expect us to join your flock," replied one of the Wild Goats. "We know how you would treat us later on if some strangers should come as we did."

It is unwise to treat old friends badly for the sake of new ones.

Copywork

Literature

"I can see the marks of little dirty feet."

Peasant Women Planting Stakes by Camille Pissarro

Picture Study

1. Read the title and the name of the artist. Study the picture for several minutes, then put the picture away.

2. Describe the picture.

3. Look at the picture again. Do you notice any details that you missed before? What do you like or dislike about this painting? Does it remind you of anything?

9. Introducing Commas; Picture Study: Peasant Women Planting Stakes

- The Tale of Johnny Town-mouse by Beatrix Potter

There's another little punctuation mark that you've probably seen in your books. It's called a **comma**, and it looks like this:

,

We use commas when we want to show a brief pause. Listen to this sentence and see if you can hear the pauses when you get to the commas.

"Never mind, they don't belong to us," said Johnny.

A Good Play

By Robert Louis Stevenson

We built a ship upon the stairs
All made of the back-bedroom chairs,
And filled it full of soft pillows
To go a-sailing on the billows.

We took a saw and several nails,
And water in the nursery pails;
And Tom said, "Let us also take
An apple and a slice of cake;"—
Which was enough for Tom and me
To go a-sailing on, till tea.

We sailed along for days and days,
And had the very best of plays;
But Tom fell out and hurt his knee,
So there was no one left but me.

Copywork

Literature

"When it rains, I sit in my little sandy burrow."

10. Introducing Exclamation Marks

- The Tale of Two Bad Mice by Beatrix Potter

So far, all of the sentences you've had for copywork ended with a period, but there are other punctuation marks that can end sentences. One is an exclamation mark. It looks like this:

!

An exclamation mark is used to show sudden or strong feeling. It can be used when someone is surprised, mad, or very happy. Anytime a sentence shows some strong emotion or surprise, an exclamation mark can be used instead of a period. Look at this sentence from "The Tale of Two Bad Mice":

What a sight met the eyes of Jane and Lucinda!

In this sentence, the exclamation mark shows us that Jane and Lucinda were very surprised!

Dusk in June

By Sara Teasdale

Evening, and all the birds
In a chorus of shimmering sound
Are easing their hearts of joy
For miles around.

The air is blue and sweet,
The few first stars are white,
Oh let me like the birds
Sing before night.

The Travelers and the Purse

An Aesop's Fable

Two men were traveling in company along the road when one of them picked up a well-filled purse.

"How lucky I am!" he said. "I have found a purse. Judging by its weight, it must be full of gold."

"Do not say 'I have found a purse,'" said his companion. "Say rather 'we have found a purse' and 'how lucky we are.' Travelers ought to share alike the fortunes or misfortunes of the road."

"No, no," replied the other angrily. "I found it, and I am going to keep it."

Just then they heard a shout of, "Stop, thief!" and, looking around, saw a mob of people armed with clubs coming down the road.

The man who had found the purse fell into a panic.

"We are lost if they find the purse on us," he cried.

"No, no," replied the other, "You would not say 'we' before, so now stick to your 'I.' Say 'I am lost.'"

We cannot expect anyone to share our misfortunes unless we are willing to share our good fortune also.

Copywork

Literature

What a sight met the eyes of Jane and Lucinda!

11. Commas

- The Tale of the Flopsy Bunnies by Beatrix Potter

Remember that we use commas when we want to show a brief pause, such as between numbers when we're counting. Point out the commas in your copywork for today:

"One, two, three, four, five, six little fat rabbits!"

In "The Tale of the Flopsy Bunnies," Mr. McGregor does a great deal of counting bunnies. How many bunnies did he actually have?

Notice that in this sentence, you have quotation marks and an exclamation mark. Mr. McGregor is speaking, and he is also excited about his catch.

The Orchard

By Walter de la Mare

Someone is always sitting there,
    In the little green orchard;
Even when the sun is high
In noon's unclouded sky,
And faintly droning goes
The bee from rose to rose,
Some one in shadow is sitting there
    In the little green orchard.

Yes, when the twilight's falling softly
    In the little green orchard;
When the grey dew distills
And every flower-cup fills;
When the last blackbird says,
'What—what!' and goes her way—ssh!
I have heard voices calling softly
    In the little green orchard.

Not that I am afraid of being there,
    In the little green orchard;
Why, when the moon's been bright,
Shedding her lonesome light,
And moths like ghosties come,
And the horned snail leaves home:
I've sat there, whispering and listening there,
    In the little green orchard.

Only it's strange to be feeling there,
    In the little green orchard;
Whether you paint or draw,
Dig, hammer, chop or saw;
When you are most alone,
All but the silence gone
Some one is watching and waiting there,
    In the little green orchard.

The Cat and the Birds

An Aesop's Fable

A Cat was growing very thin. As you have guessed, he did not get enough to eat.
One day he heard that some Birds in the neighborhood were ailing and needed a
doctor. So he put on a pair of spectacles, and, with a leather box in his hand, knocked
at the door of the Bird's home.

The Birds peeped out, and Dr. Cat, with much solicitude, asked how they were. He
would be very happy to give them some medicine.

"Tweet, tweet," laughed the Birds. "Very smart, aren't you? We are very well, thank
you, and more so, if you only keep away from here."

Be wise and shun the quack.

Copywork

Literature

"One, two, three, four, five, six little fat rabbits!"

12. Picture Narration: The Spendthrift and the Swallow

- The Tale of Jemima Puddle-duck by Beatrix Potter

The Spendthrift and the Swallow

An Aesop's Fable

A young fellow, who was very popular among his boon companions as a good spender, quickly wasted his fortune trying to live up to his reputation. Then one fine day in early spring, he found himself with not a penny left and no property save the clothes he wore.

He was to meet some jolly young men that morning, and he was at his wits' end how to get enough money to keep up appearances.

Just then a Swallow flew by, twittering merrily, and the young man, thinking summer had come, hastened off to a clothes dealer, to whom he sold all the clothes he wore down to his very tunic.

A few days later, a change in weather brought a severe frost; and the poor swallow and that foolish young man in his light tunic, and with his arms and knees bare, could scarcely keep life in their shivering bodies.

One swallow does not make a summer.

The Rainbow

By Christina G. Rossetti

Boats sail on the rivers,
And ships sail on the seas;
But clouds that sail across the sky
Are prettier than these.

There are bridges on the rivers,
As pretty as you please;
But the bow that bridges heaven,
And overtops the trees,

And builds a road from earth to sky,
Is prettier far than these.

Copywork

Literature

> She thought that it looked a safe quiet spot.

Picture Narration

Draw a picture of the Aesop's fable from today. Show your picture to your instructor and tell her about it.

13. Titles of Respect

- The Story of Miss Moppet by Beatrix Potter

Do you remember learning about titles of respect? **Mister** is a title of respect for a man. We write it as **Mr.**, which is an abbreviation. That means it's a word that we've made shorter. Abbreviations have a period at the end, which is why we put a period at the end of **Mr.** A title of respect for a married lady is **Mrs.** It's also an abbreviation.

A title of respect for a lady who is not married is **Miss**. **Miss** doesn't have a period at the end because it is not an abbreviation. When we write **Miss**, we write the whole word every time.

Nod

By Walter de la Mare

Softly along the road of evening,
In a twilight dim with rose,
Wrinkled with age, and drenched with dew,
Old Nod the shepherd goes.

His drowsy flock streams on before him,
Their fleeces charged with gold,
To where the sun's last beam leans low
On Nod the shepherds fold.

The hedge is quick and green with brier,
From their sand the conies creep;
And all the birds that fly in heaven
Flock singing home to sleep.

His lambs outnumber a noon's roses,
Yet, when night shadows fall,
His blind old sheep-dog, Slumber-soon,
Misses not one of all.

His are the quiet steps of dreamland,
The waters of no more pain,
His ram's bell rings 'neath an arch of stars,
"Rest, rest, and rest again."

The Farmer and the Snake

An Aesop's Fable

A Farmer walked through his field one cold winter morning. On the ground lay a Snake, stiff and frozen with the cold. The Farmer knew how deadly the Snake could be, and yet he picked it up and put it in his bosom to warm it back to life.

The Snake soon revived, and when it had enough strength, bit the man who had been so kind to it. The bite was deadly, and the Farmer felt that he must die. As he drew his last breath, he said to those standing around:

Learn from my fate not to take pity on a scoundrel.

Copywork

Literature

Miss Moppet jumps upon the Mouse!

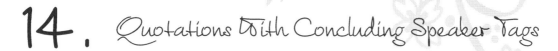

14. Quotations With Concluding Speaker Tags

- The Tale of Tom Kitten by Beatrix Potter

Often when we see a quotation, we also see a few words outside of the quotation marks which tell us who was speaking. Look at the sentence below from "The Tale of Tom Kitten":

"Let us climb up the rockery," said Moppet.

Commas are used to show a pause. They can also be used to separate a quotation from the rest of the sentence. Instead of a period, a comma was used above so that the author could tell us who was speaking.

The Land of Nod

By Robert Louis Stevenson

From breakfast on through all the day
At home among my friends I stay,
But every night I go abroad
Afar into the land of Nod.

All by myself I have to go,
With none to tell me what to do—
All alone beside the streams
And up the mountain-sides of dreams.

The strangest things are these for me,
Both things to eat and things to see,
And many frightening sights abroad
Till morning in the land of Nod.

Try as I like to find the way,
I never can get back by day,
Nor can remember plain and clear
The curious music that I hear.

The Sick Stag

An Aesop's Fable

    A Stag had fallen sick. He had just strength enough to gather some food and find a quiet clearing in the woods, where he lay down to wait until his strength should return. The Animals heard about the Stag's illness and came to ask after his health. Of course, they were all hungry and helped themselves freely to the Stag's food; and as you would expect, the Stag soon starved to death.

    Good will is worth nothing unless it is accompanied by good acts.

Copywork

Literature

       "Let us climb up the rockery," said Moppet.

Village Corner by Camille Pissarro

15. Commas in Quotations

• The Tale of Pigling Bland by Beatrix Potter

A comma can be used to separate a quotation from the rest of the sentence in order to tell us who is saying the quotation. Look at this sentence from "The Tale of Pigling Bland":

> "I wish I could have a little garden and grow potatoes," said Pigling Bland.

A comma always follows along behind a friend. It stays right with the word it follows. If the word that it follows is inside the quotation marks, the comma will be, too! Look at the sentence above again. Point out the comma, and see how it stays with its friend inside the quotation marks.

I Caught a Little Ladybird

By Christina G. Rossetti

I caught a little ladybird
That flies far away;
I caught a little lady wife
That is both staid and gay.

Come back, my scarlet ladybird,
Back from far away;
I weary of my dolly wife,
My wife that cannot play.

She's such a senseless wooden thing
She stares the livelong day;
Her wig of gold is stiff and cold
And cannot change to grey.

Copywork

"I shall after supper," said Pig-wig.

16. Introducing Question Marks

- The Tale of Timmy Tiptoes by Beatrix Potter

You've learned that you can end a sentence with either a period or an exclamation mark, but there's one more punctuation mark that can end a sentence! Do you know what it is? It looks like this:

?

It's called a question mark, and we use it to show that someone has asked a question. Look at these sentences from "The Tale of Timmy Tiptoes":

> "How shall you ever get them out again? It is like a money box!" said Goody.

Goody says two sentences in this quotation. First she asks a question, and then she says an exclamation!

Hopping Frog
By Christina G. Rossetti

Hopping frog, hop here and be seen,
I'll not pelt you with stick or stone:
Your cap is laced and your coat is green;
Good bye, we'll let each other alone.

Plodding toad, plod here and be looked at,
You the finger of scorn is crooked at:
But though you're lumpish, you're harmless too;
You won't hurt me, and I won't hurt you.

The Dog and the Oyster

An Aesop's Fable

There was once a Dog who was very fond of eggs. He visited the hen house very often and at last got so greedy that he would swallow the eggs whole.

One day the Dog wandered down to the seashore. There he spied an Oyster. In a twinkling the Oyster was resting in the Dog's stomach, shell and all.

It pained the Dog a good deal, as you can guess.

"I've learned that all round things are not eggs," he said, groaning.

Act in haste and repent at leisure——and often in pain.

Copywork

Literature

"Who's been digging up my nuts?"

17. Exclamations and Questions in Quotations

• The Roly Poly Pudding by Beatrix Potter

Sometimes, we may have someone in a story exclaiming something or asking a question. When that happens, we don't use a comma to separate the quotation from the rest of the sentence. Instead, we use an exclamation mark or a question mark. Look at this sentence from "The Roly Poly Pudding":

> "Shall we make dear little muffins?" said Mittens to Moppet.

Quotation marks show us what words Mittens said to Moppet. Mittens asked a question, so the quotation ends with a question mark followed by the ending quotation mark. Point out the question mark and the quotation marks in that sentence. Do you see that the question mark comes before the ending quotation mark?

The Kitten and the Falling Leaves

By William Wordsworth

See the kitten on the wall, sporting with the leaves that fall,
Withered leaves—one—two—and three, from the lofty elder-tree!
Through the calm and frosty air, of this morning bright and fair . . .
—But the kitten, how she starts; Crouches, stretches, paws, and darts!

First at one, and then its fellow, just as light and just as yellow;
There are many now—now one—now they stop and there are none;
What intenseness of desire, in her upward eye of fire!

With a tiger-leap half way, now she meets the coming prey,
Lets it go as fast, and then, has it in her power again:
Now she works with three or four, like an Indian Conjuror;
Quick as he in feats of art, far beyond in joy of heart.

Three Bullocks and a Lion

An Aesop's Fable

A Lion had been watching three Bullocks feeding in an open field. He had tried to attack them several times, but they had kept together and helped each other to drive him off. The Lion had little hope of eating them, for he was no match for three strong Bullocks with their sharp horns and hoofs. But he could not keep away from that field, for it is hard to resist watching a good meal, even when there is little chance of getting it.

Then one day the Bullocks had a quarrel, and when the hungry Lion came to look at them and lick his chops as he was accustomed to do, he found them in separate corners of the field, as far away from one another as they could get.

It was now an easy matter for the Lion to attack them one at a time, and this he proceeded to do with the greatest satisfaction and relish.

In unity is strength.

Copywork

Literature

"Which way did she go, Moppet?"

18. Picture Narration: The Birds, the Beasts, and the Bat

- The Pie and the Patty-pan by Beatrix Potter

The Birds, the Beasts, and the Bat

An Aesop's Fable

The Birds and the Beasts declared war against each other. No compromise was possible, and so they went at it tooth and claw. It is said the quarrel grew out of the persecution the race of Geese suffered at the teeth of the Fox family. The Beasts, too, had cause for fight. The Eagle was constantly pouncing on the Hare, and the Owl dined daily on Mice.

It was a terrible battle. Many a Hare and many a Mouse died. Chickens and Geese fell by the score—and the victor always stopped for a feast.

Now the Bat family had not openly joined either side. They were a very politic race. So when they saw the Birds getting the better of it, they were Birds for all there was in it. But when the tide of battle turned, they immediately sided with the Beasts.

When the battle was over, the conduct of the Bats was discussed at the peace conference. Such deceit was unpardonable, and Birds and Beasts made common cause to drive out the Bats. And since then the Bat family hides in dark towers and deserted ruins, flying out only in the night.

The deceitful have no friends.

Bread and Cherries

By Walter de la Mare

"Cherries, ripe cherries!"
   The old woman cried,
In her snowy white apron,
   And basket beside;
And the little boys came,
   Eyes shining, cheeks red,

To buy a bag of cherries,
    To eat with their bread.

Copywork

Literature

"Shall I run for the doctor?"

Picture Narration

Draw a picture of the Aesop's fable from today. Show your picture to your instructor and tell her about it.

19. Introducing Poetry Mechanics

• Ginger and Pickles by Beatrix Potter

Today we're going to add some poetry to your copywork! You'll write one line from a poem at a time until it's finished.

A sentence starts with a capital letter. A name starts with a capital letter. And every line of a poem starts with a capital letter.

The poem you will be copying is "The Falling Star" by Sara Teasdale. Look at it below. Point to the capital letter at the beginning of every line.

The Falling Star

By Sara Teasdale

I saw a star slide down the sky,
Blinding the north as it went by,
Too burning and too quick to hold,
Too lovely to be bought or sold,
Good only to make wishes on
And then forever to be gone.

The Fox and the Crab

An Aesop's Fable

A Crab one day grew disgusted with the sands in which he lived. He decided to take a stroll to the meadow not far inland. There he would find better fare than briny water and sand mites. So off he crawled to the meadow. But there a hungry Fox spied him and, in a twinkling, ate him up, both shell and claw.

Be content with your lot.

Copywork

Literature

"This is the last straw," said Pickles.

Poetry—The Falling Star

I saw a star slide down the sky,

20. Quotations With Beginning Speaker Tags

- The Story of a Fierce Bad Rabbit by Beatrix Potter

Sometimes an author tells us something about a quotation before the quotation! Then we use a comma to separate the quotation from the rest of the sentence. The comma comes before the beginning quotation mark. Look at the sentences below from "The Story of a Fierce Bad Rabbit." Point out all the punctuation marks.

He does not say, "Please." He takes it!

The Little Bird

By Water de la Mare

My dear Daddie bought a mansion
   For to bring my Mammie to,
In a hat with a long feather,
   And a trailing gown of blue;
And a company of fiddlers
   And a rout of maids and men
Danced the clock round to the morning,
   In a gay house-warming then.
And when all the guests were gone, and
   All was still as still can be,
In from the dark ivy hopped a
   Wee small bird: and that was Me.

The Frog and the Mouse

An Aesop's Fable

A young Mouse in search of adventure was running along the bank of a pond where lived a Frog. When the Frog saw the Mouse, he swam to the bank and croaked, "Won't you pay me a visit? I can promise you a good time if you do."

The Mouse did not need much coaxing, for he was very anxious to see the world and everything in it. But though he could swim a little, he did not dare risk going into the pond without some help.

The Frog had a plan. He tied the Mouse's leg to his own with a tough reed. Then into the pond he jumped, dragging his foolish companion with him.

The Mouse soon had enough of it and wanted to return to shore; but the treacherous Frog had other plans. He pulled the Mouse down under the water and drowned him. But before he could untie the reed that bound him to the dead Mouse, a Hawk came sailing over the pond. Seeing the body of the Mouse floating on the water, the Hawk swooped down, seized the Mouse, and carried it off with the Frog dangling from its leg. Thus at one swoop, he had caught both meat and fish for his dinner.

Those who seek to harm others often come to harm themselves through their own deceit.

Copywork

Literature

He does not say, "Please." He takes it!

Pere Gallien's House at Pontoise by Camille Pissarro

Picture Study

1. Read the title and the name of the artist. Study the picture for several minutes, then put the picture away.

2. Describe the picture.

3. Look at the picture again. Do you notice any details that you missed before? What do you like or dislike about this painting? Does it remind you of anything?

21. Punctuation Marks; Picture Study: Pere Gallien's House at Pontoise

• Just So Stories by Rudyard Kipling: How the Whale Got His Throat

Look at your copywork from How the "Whale Got His Throat" below. Point out all of the different punctuation marks in the sentences.

> "No," said the Whale. "What is it like?"

Do you know why Whale starts with a capital letter? Kipling uses the word as if it's also the animal's name! Aesop does the same in his fables.

System

By Robert Louis Stevenson

Every night my prayers I say,
And get my dinner every day;
And every day that I've been good,
I get an orange after food.

The child that is not clean and neat,
With lots of toys and things to eat,
He is a naughty child, I'm sure—
Or else his dear papa is poor.

Copywork

Literature

> "No," said the Whale. "What is it like?"

22. Introducing Vowels

- Just So Stories: How the Camel Got His Hump

The vowels are a, e, i, o, u, and sometimes y.

When you were learning to read, did you memorize the vowels? If not, you should start memorizing them now. The vowels are **a, e, i, o, u,** and sometimes **y.** Say that three times to begin memorizing the list.

What does "and sometimes y" mean? **Y** is a tricky fellow. Sometimes he says /y/ as in **yellow**. But sometimes, he says /ĭ/ as in **gym**, /ī/ as in **sky**, or /ē/ as in **baby**. When he says /ĭ/ or /ī/ or /ē/, he's acting like a vowel!

All of the other letters are called **consonants**.

You're writing another line of "The Falling Star" by Sara Teasdale today. Remember that every line of a poem begins with a capital letter!

Lullaby of an Indian Chief

By Sir Walter Scott

O hush thee, my baby, thy sire was a knight,
Thy mother a lady, both lovely and bright;
The woods and the glens, from the towers which we see,
They all are belonging, dear baby, to thee.
O ho ro, i ri ri, cadul gu lo,
O ho ro, i ri ri, cadul gu lo.

O fear not the bugle, though loudly it blows,
It calls but the warders that guard thy repose;
Their bows would be bended, their blades would be red,
Ere the step of a foeman drew near to thy bed.
O ho ro, i ri ri, cadul gu lo,
O ho ro, i ri ri, cadul gu lo.

O hush thee, my baby, the time soon will come
When thy sleep shall be broken by trumpet and drum;
Then hush thee, my darling, take rest while you may,

For strife comes with manhood, and waking with day.
O ho ro, i ri ri, cadul gu lo,
O ho ro, i ri ri, cadul gu lo.

The Serpent and the Eagle

An Aesop's Fable

A Serpent had succeeded in surprising an Eagle and had wrapped himself around the Eagle's neck. The Eagle could not reach the Serpent, neither with beak nor claws. Far into the sky he soared trying to shake off his enemy. But the Serpent's hold only tightened, and slowly the Eagle sank back to earth, gasping for breath.

A Countryman chanced to see the unequal combat. In pity for the noble Eagle, he rushed up and soon had loosened the coiling Serpent and freed the Eagle.

The Serpent was furious. He had no chance to bite the watchful Countryman. Instead he struck at the drinking horn, hanging at the Countryman's belt, and into it let fly the poison of his fangs.

The Countryman now went on toward home. Becoming thirsty on the way, he filled his horn at a spring and was about to drink.

There was a sudden rush of great wings. Sweeping down, the Eagle seized the poisoned horn from out his savior's hands and flew away with it to hide it where it could never be found.

An act of kindness is well repaid.

Copywork

Literature

"Come out and trot like the rest of us."

Poetry—The Falling Star

Blinding the north as it went by,

23. Vowels

- Just So Stories: How the Rhinoceros Got His Skin
(Note: Please see the note at the beginning of Lesson 24 before reading the next story, "How the Leopard Got His Spots.")

The vowels are a, e, i, o, u, and sometimes y.

Say the vowels three times today. If you say them three times every lesson time, you'll have them memorized very quickly.

Away to the River

By Leroy F. Jackson

Away to the river, away to the wood,
While the grasses are green and the berries are good!
Where the locusts are scraping their fiddles and bows,
And the bees keep a-coming wherever one goes.

Oh, it's off to the river and off to the hills,
To the land of the bloodroot and wild daffodils,
With a buttercup blossom to color my chin,
And a basket of burs to put sandberries in.

The Wolf in Sheep's Clothing

An Aesop's Fable

A certain Wolf could not get enough to eat because of the watchfulness of the Shepherds. But one night he found a sheep skin that had been cast aside and forgotten. The next day, dressed in the skin, the Wolf strolled into the pasture with the Sheep. Soon a little Lamb was following him about and was quickly led away to slaughter.

That evening the Wolf entered the fold with the flock. But it happened that the Shepherd took a fancy for mutton broth that very evening, and, picking up a knife, went to the fold. There the first he laid hands on and killed was the Wolf.

The evil doer often comes to harm through his own deceit.

Copywork

Literature

It tickled like cake crumbs in bed.

24. Picture Narration: The Eagle and the Jackdaw

- Just So Stories: How the Leopard Got His Spots
(Note: This story contains a racial slur in the fourth paragraph from the end of the story. Many newer versions of these stories have removed or changed this line.)

The Eagle and the Jackdaw

An Aesop's Fable

An Eagle, swooping down on powerful wings, seized a lamb in her talons and made off with it to her nest. A Jackdaw saw the deed, and his silly head was filled with the idea that he was big and strong enough to do as the Eagle had done. So with much rustling of feathers and a fierce air, he came down swiftly on the back of a large Ram. But when he tried to rise again, he found that he could not get away, for his claws were tangled in the wool. And so far was he from carrying away the Ram, that the Ram hardly noticed he was there.

The Shepherd saw the fluttering Jackdaw and at once guessed what had happened. Running up, he caught the bird and clipped its wings. That evening he gave the Jackdaw to his children.

"What a funny bird this is!" they said, laughing. "What do you call it, father?"

"That is a Jackdaw, my children. But if you should ask him, he would say he is an Eagle."

Do not let your vanity make you overestimate your powers.

Fable

By Ralph Waldo Emerson

The mountain and the squirrel
Had a quarrel;
And the former called the latter "Little Prig."
Bun replied,
"You are doubtless very big;
But all sorts of things and weather

Must be taken in together
To make up a year
And a sphere.
And I think it's no disgrace
To occupy my place.
If I'm not so large as you,
You are not so small as I,
And not half so spry.
I'll not deny you make
A very pretty squirrel track;
Talents differ: all is well and wisely put;
If I cannot carry forests on my back,
Neither can you crack a nut."

Copywork

Literature

And Baviaan winked. He knew.

Picture Narration

Draw a picture of the Aesop's fable from today. Show your picture to your instructor and tell her about it.

25. Vowels

- Just So Stories: The Elephant's Child

The vowels are a, e, i, o, u, and sometimes y.

Say the vowels three times today. Do you remember when **y** is a vowel? **Y** is a vowel when it sounds like a vowel. When it says /y/, it's acting as a consonant.

You're writing another line of the poem "The Falling Star" today. Remember that every line of a poem begins with a capital letter!

The Duel

By Eugene Field

The gingham dog and the calico cat
Side by side on the table sat;
'Twas half-past twelve, and (what do you think!)
Nor one nor t'other had slept a wink!
The old Dutch clock and the Chinese plate
Appeared to know as sure as fate
There was going to be a terrible spat.
(I wasn't there; I simply state
What was told to me by the Chinese plate!)

The gingham dog went "bow-wow-wow!"
And the calico cat replied "mee-ow!"
The air was littered, an hour or so,
With bits of gingham and calico,
While the old Dutch clock in the chimney-place
Up with its hands before its face,
For it always dreaded a family row!
(Never mind: I'm only telling you
What the old Dutch clock declares is true!)

The Chinese plate looked very blue,
And wailed, "Oh, dear! what shall we do!"

But the gingham dog and the calico cat
Wallowed this way and tumbled that,
Employing every tooth and claw
In the awfullest way you ever saw
And, oh! how the gingham and calico flew!
(Don't fancy I exaggerate
I got my news from the Chinese plate!)

Next morning where the two had sat
They found no trace of dog or cat;
And some folks think unto this day
That burglars stole that pair away!
But the truth about the cat and pup
Is this: they ate each other up!
Now what do you really think of that!
(The old Dutch clock it told me so,
And that is how I came to know.)

The Gnat and the Bull

An Aesop's Fable

A Gnat flew over the meadow, with much buzzing for so small a creature, and settled on the tip of one of the horns of a Bull. After he had rested a short time, he made ready to fly away. But before he left, he begged the Bull's pardon for having used his horn for a resting place.

"You must be very glad to have me go now," he said.

"It's all the same to me," replied the Bull. "I did not even know you were there."

We are often of greater importance in our own eyes than in the eyes of our neighbor.

The smaller the mind, the greater the conceit.

Copywork

Literature

"Come hither, Little One," said the Crocodile.

Poetry—The Falling Star

Too burning and too quick to hold,

26.  Vowels and Indefinite Articles

• Just So Stories: The Sing-Song of Old Man Kangaroo

The vowels are a, e, i, o, u, and sometimes y.

There are two little words that you use so often you probably don't even notice them. They are **a** and **an**. You might ask your mother for **an** apple or **a** banana. They mean the same thing, so why do we need both? Why can't we always just use **a**?

We need **an** to help with words that begin with vowels! When a word begins with a vowel, it's easier to say **an** than **a** in front of it. Look at the two sentences below from "The Sing-Song of Old Man Kangaroo":

He danced on <u>an</u> outcrop in the middle
of Australia.

He danced on <u>a</u> rock-ledge in the middle
of Australia.

He danced on **an** outcrop and **a** rock-ledge. **Outcrop** begins with a vowel, so we use **an**! When you're doing your copywork, look for the little words **a** and **an**. See which one the author used, and look at the word that comes after it to see why he chose that little word.

The Cat of Cats

By William Brighty Rands

I am the cat of cats. I am
The everlasting cat!
Cunning, and old, and sleek as jam,
The everlasting cat!
I hunt vermin in the night—
The everlasting cat!

For I see best without the light—
The everlasting cat!

The Donkey and the Lap Dog
An Aesop's Fable

There was once a Donkey whose Master also owned a Lap Dog. This Dog was a favorite and received many a pat and kind word from his Master, as well as choice bits from his plate. Every day the Dog would run to meet the Master, frisking playfully about and leaping up to lick his hands and face.

All this the Donkey saw with much discontent. Though he was well fed, he had much work to do; besides, the Master hardly ever took any notice of him.

Now the jealous Donkey got it into his silly head that all he had to do to win his Master's favor was to act like the Dog. So one day he left his stable and clattered eagerly into the house.

Finding his Master seated at the dinner table, he kicked up his heels and, with a loud bray, pranced giddily around the table, upsetting it as he did so. Then he planted his forefeet on his Master's knees and rolled out his tongue to lick the Master's face, as he had seen the Dog do. But his weight upset the chair, and Donkey and man rolled over together in the pile of broken dishes from the table.

The Master was much alarmed at the strange behavior of the Donkey, and calling for help, soon attracted the attention of the servants. When they saw the danger the Master was in from the clumsy beast, they set upon the Donkey and drove him with kicks and blows back to the stable. There they left him to mourn the foolishness that had brought him nothing but a sound beating.

Behavior that is regarded as agreeable in one is very rude and impertinent in another.

Do not try to gain favor by acting in a way that is contrary to your own nature and character.

Copywork

Literature

"Do you see that gentleman dancing on an ash pit?"

Place du Theatre Francais by Camille Pissarro

Picture Study

1. Read the title and the name of the artist. Study the picture for several minutes, then put the picture away.

2. Describe the picture.

3. Look at the picture again. Do you notice any details that you missed before? What do you like or dislike about this painting? Does it remind you of anything?

27. Vowels and Indefinite Articles; Picture Study: Place du Theatre Francais

- Just So Stories: The Beginning of the Armadillos

The vowels are a, e, i, o, u, and sometimes y.

Do you remember when to use **a** and when to use **an**? A comes before a word that begins with a consonant, and **an** comes before a word that begins with a vowel. Look at the sentence below from "The Beginning of the Armadillos." Can you explain why he use **a** instead of **an** in this sentence?

> "My son, when you find _a_ Hedgehog you must drop him into the water and then he will uncoil, and when you catch _a_ Tortoise you must scoop him out of his shell with your paw.'"

Our Little Pat

By Leroy F. Jackson

Our little Pat
Was chasing the cat
And kicking the kittens about.
When mother said "Quit!"
He ran off to sit
On the top of the woodpile and pout;
But a sly little grin
Soon slid down his chin
And let all the sulkiness out.

Copywork

Literature

And he had a friend, a Slow-Solid Tortoise.

28. Exclamation Marks

- Just So Stories: How the First Letter Was Written

Do you remember why we use an exclamation mark?

!

An exclamation mark is used to show sudden or strong feeling. It can show surprise, happiness, anger, or any other feeling that is strong or sudden.

The Duck and the Kangaroo

By Edward Lear

Said the Duck to the Kangaroo,
'Good gracious! How you hop!
Over the fields and the water too,
As if you never would stop!
My life is a bore in this nasty pond,
And I long to go out in the world beyond!
I wish I could hop like you!'
Said the Duck to the Kangaroo.

'Please give me a ride on your back!'
Said the Duck to the Kangaroo.
'I would sit quite still, and say nothing but "quack,"
The whole of the long day through!
And we'd go to the Dee, and the Jelly Bo Lee,
Over the land and over the sea;
Please take me a ride! O do!'
Said the Duck to the Kangaroo.

Said the Kangaroo to the Duck,
'This requires some little reflection;
Perhaps on the whole it might bring me luck,
And there seems but one objection,

Which is, if you'll let me speak so bold,
Your feet are unpleasantly wet and cold,
And would probably give me the roo-
Matiz!' said the Kangaroo.

Said the Duck, 'As I sat on the rocks,
I have thought over that completely,
And I bought four pairs of worsted socks
Which fit my web feet neatly.
And to keep out the cold I've bought a cloak,
And every day a cigar I'll smoke,
All to follow my own dear true
Love of a Kangaroo?'

Said the Kangaroo, 'I'm ready!
All in the moonlight pale;
But to balance me well, dear Duck, sit steady!
And quite at the end of my tail!'
So away they went with a hop and a bound,
And they hopped the whole world three times round;
And who so happy, O who,
As the Duck and the Kangaroo?

The Bull and the Goat

An Aesop's Fable

A Bull once escaped from a Lion by entering a cave which the Goatherds used to house their flocks in stormy weather and at night. It happened that one of the Goats had been left behind, and the Bull had no sooner got inside than this Goat lowered his head and made a rush at him, butting him with his horns. As the Lion was still prowling outside the entrance to the cave, the Bull had to submit to the insult.

"Do not think," he said, "that I submit to your cowardly treatment because I am afraid of you. When that Lion leaves, I'll teach you a lesson you won't forget."

It is wicked to take advantage of another's distress.

Copywork

Literature

Now attend and listen!

Poetry—The Falling Star

Too lovely to be bought or sold,

29. Review

- Just So Stories: How the Alphabet Was Made

Can you recite the vowels without help?

The vowels are **a, e, i, o, u**, and sometimes **y**.

Can you remember when **y** is a vowel?

Y is a vowel when it sounds like a vowel! **Y** appears twice in your copywork sentence today. Let's look at the sentence:

Her Daddy said, "Don't be silly, child."

Point out each **y** in the sentence. Is it acting as a vowel or as a consonant? Can you explain why?

A Cradle Song

By Thomas Dekker

Golden slumbers kiss your eyes,
Smiles awake you when you rise.
Sleep, pretty wantons, do not cry,
And I will sing a lullaby:
Rock them, rock them, lullaby.

Care is heavy, therefore sleep you;
You are care, and care must keep you.
Sleep, pretty wantons, do not cry,
And I will sing a lullaby:
Rock them, rock them, lullaby.

The Old Lion and the Fox

An Aesop's Fable

An old Lion, whose teeth and claws were so worn that it was not so easy for him to get food as in his younger days, pretended that he was sick. He took care to let all his neighbors know about it, and then he lay down in his cave to wait for visitors. And when they came to offer him their sympathy, he ate them up one by one.

The Fox came too, but he was very cautious about it. Standing at a safe distance from the cave, he inquired politely after the Lion's health. The Lion replied that he was very ill indeed and asked the Fox to step in for a moment. But Master Fox very wisely stayed outside, thanking the Lion very kindly for the invitation.

"I should be glad to do as you ask," he added, "but I have noticed that there are many footprints leading into your cave and none coming out. Pray tell me, how do your visitors find their way out again?"

Take warning from the misfortunes of others.

Copywork

Literature

Her Daddy said, "Don't be silly, child."

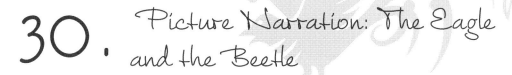

30. Picture Narration: The Eagle and the Beetle

- Just So Stories: The Crab That Played With the Sea

The Eagle and the Beetle

An Aesop's Fable

A Beetle once begged the Eagle to spare a Hare which had run to her for protection. But the Eagle pounced upon her prey, the sweep of her great wings tumbling the Beetle a dozen feet away. Furious at the disrespect shown her, the Beetle flew to the Eagle's nest and rolled out the eggs. Not one did she spare. The Eagle's grief and anger knew no bounds, but who had done the cruel deed she did not know.

Next year the Eagle built her nest far up on a mountain crag; but the Beetle found it and again destroyed the eggs. In despair the Eagle now implored great Jupiter to let her place her eggs in his lap. There none would dare harm them. But the Beetle buzzed about Jupiter's head and made him rise to drive her away; and the eggs rolled from his lap.

Now the Beetle told the reason for her action, and Jupiter had to acknowledge the justice of her cause. And they say that ever after, while the Eagle's eggs lie in the nest in spring, the Beetle still sleeps in the ground. For so Jupiter commanded.

Even the weakest may find means to avenge a wrong.

Crumbs to the Birds

By Charles Lamb

A bird appears a thoughtless thing,
He's ever living on the wing,
And keeps up such a carolling,
That little else to do but sing
A man would guess had he.

No doubt he has his little cares,
And very hard he often fares,

The which so patiently he bears,
That, listening to those cheerful airs,
Who knows but he may be

In want of his next meal of seeds?
I think for that his sweet song pleads.
If so, his pretty art succeeds.
I'll scatter there among the weeds
All the small crumbs I see.

Copywork

Literature

"Was that well done?" said the Eldest Magician.

Picture Narration

Draw a picture of the Aesop's fable from today. Show your picture to your instructor and tell her about it.

31. Question Marks and Quotations

- Just So Stories: The Cat That Walked by Himself

We use a question mark when a question has been asked, and quotation marks wrap around the exact words that someone has said. What question does the Cat ask in the sentence below from "The Cat That Walked by Himself"?

"And if you say three words?" said the Cat.

Look closely at the punctuation marks in that sentence. Can you point to them all and name them?

Notice that the question mark comes **before** the ending quotation mark.

Don't forget to capitalize the first word when you copy the line from your poem today!

Escape at Bedtime

By Robert Louis Stevenson

The lights from the parlor and kitchen shone out
    Through the blinds and the windows and bars;
And high overhead and all moving about,
    There were thousands of millions of stars.
There ne'er were such thousands of leaves on a tree,
    Nor of people in church or the Park,
As the crowds of the stars that looked down upon me,
    And that glittered and winked in the dark.

The Dog, and the Plough, and the Hunter, and all,
    And the star of the sailor, and Mars,
These shown in the sky, and the pail by the wall
    Would be half full of water and stars.
They saw me at last, and they chased me with cries,
    And they soon had me packed into bed;
But the glory kept shining and bright in my eyes,
    And the stars going round in my head.

The Man and the Lion

An Aesop's Fable

A Lion and a Man chanced to travel in company through the forest. They soon began to quarrel, for each of them boasted that he and his kind were far superior to the other both in strength and mind.

Now they reached a clearing in the forest, and there stood a statue. It was a representation of Hercules in the act of tearing the jaws of the Nemean Lion.

"See," said the man, "that's how strong we are! The King of Beasts is like wax in our hands!"

"Ho!" laughed the Lion, "a Man made that statue. It would have been quite a different scene had a Lion made it!"

It all depends on the point of view and who tells the story.

Copywork

Literature

"And if you say three words?" said the Cat.

Poetry—The Falling Star

Good only to make wishes on

32. Quotations With Beginning Speaker Tags

• Just So Stories: The Butterfly That Stamped

Commas are used to show a pause, and they can also separate a quotation from the rest of the sentence. When an author wants to tell us something about the quote, such as who is saying it, before the quote, a comma comes before the beginning quotation mark. Look at the sentence from "The Butterfly That Stamped" and point out the commas and the quotation marks.

> And he held out his finger and said, "Little man, come here."

Mary's Little Lamb

By Sarah Josepha Hale

Mary had a little lamb,
Its fleece was white as snow;
And everywhere that Mary went,
The lamb was sure to go.
He followed her to school one day-
That was against the rule;
It made the children laugh and play,
To see a lamb at school.

So the teacher turned him out,
But still he lingered near,
And waited patiently about,
Till Mary did appear.
Then he ran to her, and laid
His head upon her arm,
As if he said, "I'm not afraid-
You'll keep me from all harm."

"What makes the lamb love Mary so?"
The eager children cry.
"Oh, Mary loves the lamb, you know,"
The teacher did reply.
"And you each gentle animal
In confidence may bind,
And make it follow at your call
If you are always kind."

The Goatherd and the Goat

An Aesop's Fable

A Goat strayed away from the flock, tempted by a patch of clover. The Goatherd tried to call it back, but in vain. It would not obey him. Then he picked up a stone and threw it, breaking the Goat's horn.

The Goatherd was frightened.

"Do not tell the master," he begged the Goat.

"No," said the Goat, "that broken horn can speak for itself!"

Wicked deeds will not stay hid.

Copywork

Literature

And he held out his finger and said, "Little man, come here."

Woman Carrying a Pitcher on Her Head by Camille Pissarro

Picture Study

1. Read the title and the name of the artist. Study the picture for several minutes, then put the picture away.

2. Describe the picture.

3. Look at the picture again. Do you notice any details that you missed before? What do you like or dislike about this painting? Does it remind you of anything?

33. Punctuation Marks; Picture Study: Woman Carrying a Pitcher on Her Head

• Five Children and It by Edith Nesbit, Chapter 1

Can you name these punctuation marks? When do we use each one?

" "   ,   !   ?   .

Quotation marks show us when someone in a story is speaking. They wrap around the words that someone says.

The comma shows a brief pause.

The exclamation mark ends a sentence and shows sudden or strong feeling.

The question mark ends a sentence and shows that a question has been asked.

The period ends all other sentences.

The Cupboard
By Walter de la Mare

I know a little cupboard,
With a teeny tiny key,
And there's a jar of Lollypops
  For me, me, me.

It has a little shelf, my dear,
As dark as dark can be,
And there's a dish of Banbury Cakes
  For me, me, me.

I have a small fat grandmamma,
With a very slippery knee,
And she's the Keeper of the Cupboard
  With the key, key, key.

And when I'm very good, my dear,
As good as good can be,
There's Banbury Cakes, and Lollypops
  For me, me, me.

Copywork

Literature

"Don't you know a Sand-fairy when you see one?"

34. Introducing Contractions

- Five Children and It, Chapter 2

Do you know what **contract** means? It means to make something smaller. Sometimes, we contract words to make them smaller. We call them **contractions**. When we make a contraction, we push the words together and we take out some of the letters. We replace the letters with a punctuation mark called an apostrophe. Look at these contractions that all have the word **not**. The **o** in **not** is replaced by an apostrophe.

"Shall not" and "will not" are tricky. They don't follow the rules!

is not	isn't	are not	aren't
was not	wasn't	were not	weren't
do not	don't	does not	doesn't
did not	didn't	have not	haven't
has not	hasn't	had not	hadn't
cannot	can't	could not	couldn't
will not	won't	would not	wouldn't
shall not	shan't	should not	shouldn't

When you do your poetry copywork, don't forget to capitalize the first word in the line from your poem!

Laughing Song
By William Blake

When the green woods laugh with the voice of joy,
And the dimpling stream runs laughing by;
When the air does laugh with our merry wit,
And the green hill laughs with the noise of it;

When the meadows laugh with lively green,
And the grasshopper laughs in the merry scene;
When Mary and Susan and Emily
With their sweet round mouths sing 'Ha ha he!'

When the painted birds laugh in the shade,
Where our table with cherries and nuts is spread:
Come live, and be merry, and join with me,
To sing the sweet chorus of 'Ha ha he!'

The Wolf and the Shepherd

An Aesop's Fable

A Wolf, lurking near the Shepherd's hut, saw the Shepherd and his family feasting on a roasted lamb.

"Aha!" he muttered. "What a great shouting and running about there would have been, had they caught me at just the very thing they are doing with so much enjoyment!"

Men often condemn others for what they see no wrong in doing themselves.

Copywork

Literature

"Don't you forget, it won't last after sunset."

Poetry—The Falling Star

And then forever to be gone.

35. Contractions

- Five Children and It, Chapter 3

Remember, when we make a contraction, we push two words together. Some of the letters are left out to make the contraction smaller, and we replace those letters with an apostrophe. Look at the contraction in the sentence below from *Five Children and It*. Which two words made up the contraction?

"It <u>doesn't</u> matter," said Robert sulkily.

The Way Through the Woods

By Rudyard Kipling

They shut the road through the woods
Seventy years ago.
Weather and rain have undone it again,
And now you would never know
There was once a path through the woods
Before they planted the trees.
It is underneath the coppice and heath,
And the thin anemonies.
Only the keeper sees
That, where the ringdove broods,
And the badgers roll at ease,
There was once a road through the woods.
Yet, if you enter the woods
Of a summer evening late,
When the night air cools on the trout-ring'd pools
Where the otter whistles his mate
(They fear not men in the woods
Because they see so few),
You will hear the beat of a horse's feet
And the swish of a skirt in the dew,
Steadily cantering through

The misty solitudes,
As though they perfectly knew
The old lost road through the woods. . . .
But there is no road through the woods.

The Farmer and the Stork

An Aesop's Fable

A Stork of a very simple and trusting nature had been asked by a gay party of Cranes to visit a field that had been newly planted. But the party ended dismally with all the birds entangled in the meshes of the Farmer's net.

The Stork begged the Farmer to spare him.

"Please let me go," he pleaded. "I belong to the Stork family who you know are honest and birds of good character. Besides, I did not know the Cranes were going to steal."

"You may be a very good bird," answered the Farmer, "but I caught you with the thieving Cranes, and you will have to share the same punishment with them."

You are judged by the company you keep.

Copywork

Literature

"It doesn't matter," said Robert sulkily.

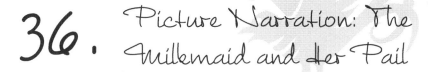

36. Picture Narration: The Milkmaid and Her Pail

• Five Children and It, Chapter 4

The Milkmaid and Her Pail

An Aesop's Fable

A Milkmaid had been out to milk the cows and was returning from the field with the shining milk pail balanced nicely on her head. As she walked along, her pretty head was busy with plans for the days to come.

"This good, rich milk," she mused, "will give me plenty of cream to churn. The butter I make I will take to market, and with the money I get for it, I will buy a lot of eggs for hatching. How nice it will be when they are all hatched and the yard is full of fine young chicks. Then when May day comes, I will sell them, and with the money I'll buy a lovely new dress to wear to the fair. All the young men will look at me. They will come and try to make love to me—but I shall very quickly send them about their business!"

As she thought of how she would settle that matter, she tossed her head scornfully, and down fell the pail of milk to the ground. And all the milk flowed out, and with it vanished butter and eggs and chicks and new dress and all the milkmaid's pride.

Do not count your chickens before they are hatched.

Song for a Little House

By Christopher Morley

I'm glad our house is a little house,
Not too tall nor too wide:
I'm glad the hovering butterflies
Feel free to come inside.

Our little house is a friendly house.
It is not shy or vain;

It gossips with the talking trees,
And makes friends with the rain.

And quick leaves cast a shimmer of green
Against our whited walls,
And in the phlox, the duteous bees
Are paying duty calls.

Copywork

Literature

"Oh, this isn't a magic wish."

Picture Narration

Draw a picture of the Aesop's fable from today. Show your picture to your
instructor and tell her about it.

37. Introducing the Days of the Week; Contractions

• Five Children and It, Chapter 5

The days of the week are Sunday, Monday, Tuesday,
Wednesday, Thursday, Friday, and Saturday.

Today we're going to begin learning the days of the week. There are seven days in the week, and your new poem to copy is a Mother Goose Rhyme to practice writing the names. Say the list three times during each lesson until you can recite them all. When you can say them all without help, then you can just recite them once. The days of the week always begin with capital letters.

"You won't believe us, but it doesn't matter."

There are two contractions in your copywork today. Point out the contractions. Which words were pushed together to make each contraction? What's the name of the punctuation mark that shows where the missing letters would go?

Don't forget: When we copy poems, we capitalize the first letter of every line. We also capitalize the names of the days of the week, just like we do for the names of people.

How Many Days

A Mother Goose Rhyme

How many days has my baby to play?
  Saturday, Sunday, Monday,
  Tuesday, Wednesday, Thursday, Friday,
  Saturday, Sunday, Monday.

The Fox and the Stork

An Aesop's Fable

The Fox one day thought of a plan to amuse himself at the expense of the Stork, at whose odd appearance he was always laughing.

"You must come and dine with me today," he said to the Stork, smiling to himself at the trick he was going to play. The Stork gladly accepted the invitation and arrived in good time and with a very good appetite.

For dinner the Fox served soup. But it was set out in a very shallow dish, and all the Stork could do was to wet the very tip of his bill. Not a drop of soup could he get. But the Fox lapped it up easily and, to increase the disappointment of the Stork, made a great show of enjoyment.

The hungry Stork was much displeased at the trick, but he was a calm, even-tempered fellow and saw no good in flying into a rage. Instead, not long afterward, he invited the Fox to dine with him in turn. The Fox arrived promptly at the time that had been set, and the Stork served a fish dinner that had a very appetizing smell. But it was served in a tall jar with a very narrow neck. The Stork could easily get at the food with his long bill, but all the Fox could do was to lick the outside of the jar and sniff at the delicious odor. And when the Fox lost his temper, the Stork said calmly:

Do not play tricks on your neighbors unless you can stand the same treatment yourself.

Copywork

Literature

"You won't believe us, but it doesn't matter."

Poetry—How Many Days

How many days has my baby to play?

38. Days of the Week; Contractions

• Five Children and It, Chapter 6

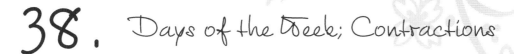

The days of the week are Sunday, Monday, Tuesday,
Wednesday, Thursday, Friday, and Saturday.

Say the days of the week three times today to help you memorize them.

Not all contractions have the word **not** in them. Here's a list of other contractions and what they mean.

I am	I'm	I will	I'll
we are	we're	we will	we'll
you are	you're	you will	you'll
he is	he's	he will	he'll
she is	she's	she will	she'll
it is	it's	it will	it'll
they are	they're	they will	they'll

It'll is a contraction, but it's not used very often.

Today, you have a new type of copywork to do— a wise saying called a maxim.

The Cow

By Robert Louis Stevenson

The friendly cow all red and white,
    I love with all my heart:
She gives me cream with all her might,
    To eat with apple-tart.

She wanders lowing here and there,
    And yet she cannot stray,

All in the pleasant open air,
   The pleasant light of day;

And blown by all the winds that pass
   And wet with all the showers,
She walks among the meadow grass
   And eats the meadow flowers.

The Wolf and the Lion

An Aesop's Fable

A Wolf had stolen a Lamb and was carrying it off to his lair to eat it. But his plans were very much changed when he met a Lion who, without making any excuses, took the Lamb away from him.

The Wolf made off to a safe distance and then said in a much injured tone, "You have no right to take my property like that!"

The Lion looked back, but as the Wolf was too far away to be taught a lesson without too much inconvenience, he said, "Your property? Did you buy it, or did the Shepherd make you a gift of it? Pray tell me, how did you get it?"

What is evil won is evil lost.

Copywork

Literature

"It's just like that Sand-fairy!"

Maxim

Actions speak louder than words.

The Swing by Pierre-Auguste Renoir

Picture Study

1. Read the title and the name of the artist. Study the picture for several minutes, then put the picture away.

2. Describe the picture.

3. Look at the picture again. Do you notice any details that you missed before? What do you like or dislike about this painting? Does it remind you of anything?

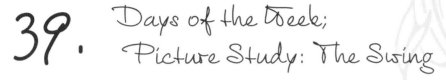

39. Days of the Week; Picture Study: The Swing

• Five Children and It, Chapter 7

The days of the week are Sunday, Monday, Tuesday,
Wednesday, Thursday, Friday, and Saturday.

Say the days of the week three times today to help you memorize them. Once you can say them without help, you need only recite the list.

Look at your copywork sentence from *Five Children and It*. Point out the contraction and the apostrophe. Remember that the apostrophe is the punctuation mark that replaces the missing letters in a contraction.

"And I'll tell the others to fetch theirs."

The Animal Show

By Leroy F. Jackson

Father and mother and Bobbie will go
To see all the sights at the animal show.
Where lions and bears
Sit on dining room chairs,
Where a camel is able
To stand on a table,
Where monkeys and seals
All travel on wheels,
And a Zulu baboon
Rides a baby balloon.
The sooner you're ready, the sooner we'll go.
Aboard, all aboard, for the Animal Show!

Copywork

Literature

"And I'll tell the others to fetch theirs."

40. Days of the Week

- Five Children and It, Chapter 8

The days of the week are Sunday, Monday, Tuesday,
Wednesday, Thursday, Friday, and Saturday.

Say the days of the week three times today to help you memorize them.

Can you remember the name of the punctuation mark that we use to replace the missing letters in a contraction? Point it out in the sentence below.

"We're wasting the whole morning."

The North Winds Blow

A Mother Goose Rhyme

Cold and raw the North winds blow
  Bleak in the morning early,
All the hills are covered with snow,
  And winter's now come fairly.

The Mice and the Weasels

An Aesop's Fable

The Weasels and the Mice were always up in arms against each other. In every battle the Weasels carried off the victory, as well as a large number of the Mice, which they ate for dinner next day. In despair the Mice called a council, and there it was decided that the Mouse army was always beaten because it had no leaders. So a large number of generals and commanders were appointed from among the most eminent Mice.

To distinguish themselves from the soldiers in the ranks, the new leaders proudly bound on their heads lofty crests and ornaments of feathers or straw. Then after long preparation of the Mouse army in all the arts of war, they sent a challenge to the Weasels.

The Weasels accepted the challenge with eagerness, for they were always ready for a fight when a meal was in sight. They immediately attacked the Mouse army in large numbers. Soon the Mouse line gave way before the attack and the whole army fled for cover. The privates easily slipped into their holes, but the Mouse leaders could not squeeze through the narrow openings because of their head-dresses. Not one escaped the teeth of the hungry Weasels.

Greatness has its penalties.

Copywork

Literature

"We're wasting the whole morning."

Poetry—How Many Days

Saturday, Sunday, Monday,

41. Days of the Week; Introducing Maxims

• Five Children and It, Chapter 9

The days of the week are Sunday, Monday, Tuesday,
Wednesday, Thursday, Friday, and Saturday.

Say the days of the week three times today to help you memorize them. Remember, once you know them, you need only recite them once.

Today you have a maxim to copy. Do you know what a maxim is? A maxim is a wise saying. Today's maxim is this:

Practice makes perfect.

That means that the more you practice at something, the better you get. That's why we say the days of the week three times each lesson, so that soon you'll know them perfectly!

Fairy Bread

By Robert Louis Stevenson

Come up here, O dusty feet!
    Here is fairy bread to eat.
Here in my retiring room,
Children, you may dine
On the golden smell of broom
    And the shade of pine;
And when you have eaten well,
Fairy stories hear and tell.

The Peacock

An Aesop's Fable

The Peacock, they say, did not at first have the beautiful feathers in which he now takes so much pride. These, Juno, whose favorite he was, granted to him one day when he begged her for a train of feathers to distinguish him from the other birds. Then, decked in his finery, gleaming with emerald, gold, purple, and azure, he strutted proudly among the birds. All regarded him with envy. Even the most beautiful pheasant could see that his beauty was surpassed.

Presently the Peacock saw an Eagle soaring high up in the blue sky and felt a desire to fly as he had been accustomed to do. Lifting his wings, he tried to rise from the ground. But the weight of his magnificent train held him down. Instead of flying up to greet the first rays of the morning sun or to bathe in the rosy light among the floating clouds at sunset, he would have to walk the ground more encumbered and oppressed than any common barnyard fowl.

Do not sacrifice your freedom for the sake of pomp and show.

Copywork

Literature

"Let's wake him up and see what he'll do."

Maxim

Practice makes perfect.

42. Picture Narration: The Hares and the Frogs

- Five Children and It, Chapter 10

The Hares and the Frogs

An Aesop's Fable

Hares, as you know, are very timid. The least shadow sends them scurrying in fright to a hiding place. Once they decided to die rather than live in such misery. But while they were debating how best to meet death, they thought they heard a noise and, in a flash, were scampering off to the warren. On the way they passed a pond where a family of Frogs was sitting among the reeds on the bank. In an instant the startled Frogs were seeking safety in the mud.

"Look," cried a Hare, "things are not so bad after all, for here are creatures who are even afraid of us!"

However unfortunate we may think we are there is always someone worse off than ourselves.

The Swing

By Robert Louis Stevenson

How do you like to go up in a swing,
Up in the air so blue?
Oh, I do think it the pleasantest thing
Ever a child can do!

Up in the air and over the wall,
Till I can see so wide,
River and trees and cattle and all
Over the countryside—

Till I look down on the garden green,
Down on the roof so brown—

Up in the air I go flying again,
Up in the air and down!

Copywork

Literature

"Don't be silly. It's a matter of life and death."

Picture Narration

Draw a picture of the Aesop's fable from today. Show your picture to your instructor and tell her about it.

43. Days of the Week

- Five Children and It, Chapter 11

The days of the week are Sunday, Monday, Tuesday, Wednesday, Thursday, Friday, and Saturday.

Say the days of the week three times today to help you memorize them, or recite them once if you know them by heart.

Mr. Nobody

Anonymous

I know a funny little man
As quiet as a mouse
He does the mischief that is done
In everybody's house.
Though no one ever sees his face
Yet one and all agree
That every plate we break was cracked
By Mr Nobody.

'Tis he who always tears our books,
Who leaves the door ajar.
He picks the buttons from our shirts
And scatters pins afar.
That squeaking door will always squeak—
For prithee, don't you see?
We leave the oiling to be done
By Mr Nobody.

He puts damp wood upon the fire
That kettles will not boil:
His are the feet that bring in mud
And all the carpets soil.

The papers that so oft are lost—
Who had them last but he?
There's no one tosses them about
But Mr Nobody.

The fingermarks upon the door
By none of us were made.
We never leave the blinds unclosed
To let the curtains fade.
The ink we never spill! The boots
That lying round you see
Are not our boots—they all belong
To Mr Nobody.

The Travelers and the Sea

An Aesop's Fable

Two Travelers were walking along the seashore. Far out they saw something riding on the waves.

"Look!" said one. "A great ship rides in from distant lands bearing rich treasures!"

The object they saw came ever nearer the shore.

"No," said the other, "that is not a treasure ship. That is some fisherman's skiff with the day's catch of savory fish."

Still nearer came the object. The waves washed it up on shore.

"It is a chest of gold lost from some wreck," they cried. Both Travelers rushed to the beach, but there they found nothing but a water-soaked log.

Do not let your hopes carry you away from reality.

Copywork

Literature

"Goodness knows what we're in for!"

Poetry—How Many Days

Tuesday, Wednesday, Thursday, Friday,

44. Review Punctuation Marks

- The Jungle Book by Rudyard Kipling: Mowgli's Brothers (first half)

Can you name these punctuation marks? When do we use each one?

" "   ,   !   ?   .

Quotation marks show us when someone in a story is speaking. They wrap around the words that someone speaks.

The comma shows a brief pause.

The exclamation mark ends a sentence and shows sudden or strong feeling.

The question mark ends a sentence and shows that a question has been asked.

The period ends all other sentences.

Where Are You Going?

By Leroy F. Jackson

Where are you going, sister Kate?
I'm going to swing on the garden gate,
And watch the fairy gypsies dance
Their tim-tam-tum on the cabbage-plants—
The great big one with the purple nose,
And the tiny tad with the pinky toes.

Where are you going, brother Ben?
I'm going to build a tiger-pen.
I'll get iron and steel and 'lectric wire
And build it a hundred feet, or higher,
And put ten tigers in it too,
And a big wildcat, and—mebbe—you.

Where are you going, mother mine?
I'm going to sit by the old grapevine,
And watch the gliding swallow bring
Clay for her nest from the meadow spring—

119

Clay and straw and a bit of thread
To weave it into a baby's bed.

Where are you going, grandma dear?
I'm going, love, where the skies are clear,
And the light winds lift the poppy flowers
And gather clouds for the summer showers,
Where the old folks and the children play
On the warm hillside through the livelong day.

The Mule

An Aesop's Fable

A Mule had had a long rest and much good feeding. He was feeling very vigorous indeed and pranced around loftily, holding his head high.

"My father certainly was a full-blooded racer," he said. "I can feel that distinctly."

Next day he was put into harness again, and that evening he was very downhearted indeed.

"I was mistaken," he said. "My father was a Donkey after all."

Be sure of your pedigree before you boast of it.

Copywork

Literature

"Enter, then, and look," said Father Wolf stiffly.

Maxim

Many hands make light work.

Camille Monet and Her Son Jean in the Garden at Argenteuil by Pierre Auguste Renoir

Picture Study

1. Read the title and the name of the artist. Study the picture for several minutes, then put the picture away.

2. Describe the picture.

3. Look at the picture again. Do you notice any details that you missed before? What do you like or dislike about this painting? Does it remind you of anything?

45. Introducing Dashes

- The Jungle Book: Mowgli's Brothers (second half),
Hunting-Song of the Seeonee Pack

Let's look at your copywork sentence for today from *The Jungle Book*:

> "He is a man—a man—a man!" snarled the Pack.

Did you notice a new punctuation mark in that sentence? It's called a dash. It's used for the same reasons as a comma. It can show a brief pause and it can separate words in a sentence. Commas are used far more frequently, however, so if you're writing something of your own and need to show a brief pause, you should use a comma.

Animal Crackers

By Christopher Morley

Animal crackers, and cocoa to drink,
That is the finest of suppers, I think;
When I'm grown up and can have what I please
I think I shall always insist upon these.

What do you choose when you're offered a treat?
When Mother says, "What would you like best to eat?"
Is it waffles and syrup, or cinnamon toast?
It's cocoa and animals that I love the most!

The kitchen's the coziest place that I know:
The kettle is singing, the stove is aglow,
And there in the twilight, how jolly to see
The cocoa and animals waiting for me.

Daddy and Mother dine later in state,
With Mary to cook for them, Susan to wait;
But they don't have nearly as much fun as I
Who eat in the kitchen with Nurse standing by;

And Daddy once said he would like to be me
Having cocoa and animals once more for tea!

Copywork

Literature

"He is a man—a man—a man!" snarled the Pack.

46. Quotations With Concluding Speaker Tags

- The Jungle Book: Kaa's Hunting (first half)

Remember that when the author says something directly after a quotation, such as who said the quote, a comma separates the quotation from the rest of the sentence. The comma always travels closely behind a friend, so it is placed inside the quotation marks just before the closing quotation mark.

"But think how small he is," said the Black Panther.

The Star

By Jane Taylor

Twinkle, twinkle, little star,
How I wonder what you are!
Up above the world so high,
Like a diamond in the sky.

When the blazing sun is gone,
When he nothing shines upon,
Then you show your little light,
Twinkle, twinkle, all the night.

Then the traveller in the dark,
Thanks you for your tiny spark,
He could not see which way to go,
If you did not twinkle so.

In the dark blue sky you keep,
And often through my curtains peep,
For you never shut your eye,
Till the sun is in the sky.

'Tis your bright and tiny spark,
Lights the traveller in the dark :
Though I know not what you are,
Twinkle, twinkle, little star.

The Dog and His Master's Dinner

An Aesop's Fable

A Dog had learned to carry his master's dinner to him every day. He was very faithful to his duty, though the smell of the good things in the basket tempted him.

The Dogs in the neighborhood noticed him carrying the basket and soon discovered what was in it. They made several attempts to steal it from him. But he always guarded it faithfully.

Then one day all the Dogs in the neighborhood got together and met him on his way with the basket. The Dog tried to run away from them. But at last he stopped to argue.

That was his mistake. They soon made him feel so ridiculous that he dropped the basket and seized a large piece of roast meat intended for his master's dinner.

"Very well," he said, "you divide the rest."

Do not stop to argue with temptation.

Copywork

Literature

"But think how small he is," said the Black Panther.

Poetry—How Many Days

Saturday, Sunday, Monday.

47. A Poem and a Fable

- The Jungle Book: Kaa's Hunting (second half),
  Road-Song of the Bandar-Log

The Fairy

By William Blake

Come hither my sparrows
My little arrows
If a tear or a smile
Will a man beguile
If an amorous delay
Clouds a sunshiny day
If the step of a foot
Smites the heart to its root
'Tis the marriage ring
Makes each fairy a king.

So a fairy sung
From the leaves I sprung
He leap'd from the spray
To flee away
But in my hat caught
He soon shall be taught
Let him laugh let him cry,
He's my butterfly
For I've pull'd out the Sting
Of the marriage ring.

The Lion and the Donkey

An Aesop's Fable

A Lion and a Donkey agreed to go hunting together. In their search for game the hunters saw a number of Wild Goats run into a cave, and they laid plans to catch them. The Donkey was to go into the cave and drive the Goats out while the Lion would stand at the entrance to strike them down.

The plan worked beautifully. The Donkey made such a frightful din in the cave, kicking and braying with all his might, that the Goats came running out in a panic of fear, only to fall victim to the Lion.

The Donkey came proudly out of the cave.

"Did you see how I made them run?" he said.

"Yes, indeed," answered the Lion, "and if I had not known you and your kind, I should certainly have run, too."

The loud-mouthed boaster does not impress nor frighten those who know him.

Copywork

Literature

"Is there yet light enough to see?"

Maxim

Waste not, want not.

48. Picture Narration: The Vain Jackdaw and His Borrowed Feathers

- The Jungle Book: "Tiger! Tiger!" (first half)

The Vain Jackdaw and His Borrowed Feathers

An Aesop's Fable

A Jackdaw chanced to fly over the garden of the King's palace. There he saw with much wonder and envy a flock of royal Peacocks in all the glory of their splendid plumage.

Now the black Jackdaw was not a very handsome bird nor very refined in manner. Yet he imagined that all he needed to make himself fit for the society of the Peacocks was a dress like theirs. So he picked up some castoff feathers of the Peacocks and stuck them among his own black plumes.

Dressed in his borrowed finery, he strutted loftily among the birds of his own kind. Then he flew down into the garden among the Peacocks. But they soon saw who he was. Angry at the cheat, they flew at him, plucking away the borrowed feathers and also some of his own.

The poor Jackdaw returned sadly to his former companions. There another unpleasant surprise awaited him. They had not forgotten his superior airs toward them, and, to punish him, they drove him away with a rain of pecks and jeers.

Borrowed feathers do not make fine birds.

Calm Morning at Sea

By Sara Teasdale

Mid-ocean like a pale blue morning-glory
Opened wide, wide;
The ship cut softly through the silken surface;
We watched white sea-birds ride
Unrocking on the holy virgin water
Fleckless on every side.

Copywork

"Are all well in the jungle?" said Mowgli, hugging him.

Picture Narration

Draw a picture of the Aesop's fable from today. Show your picture to your instructor and tell her about it.

49. Introducing the Four Seasons

- The Jungle Book: "Tiger! Tiger!" (second half), Mowgli's Song

The four seasons are winter, spring, summer, and fall.

There are four seasons in a year, and you're going to begin memorizing them. Say them three times today and every lesson day until you can recite them without help. You'll also begin copying the first stanza of your new poem. In this case, the first stanza is the first six lines.

In March, spring begins. The weather begins to get warmer, birds return from the south to start families, and hibernating animals awake. Trees grow new leaves and plants begin to bloom.

In June, summer begins. Summer is the hottest time of year. Trees are full of leaves, collecting energy from the sun.

In September, fall begins. Fall is also called autumn. The weather begins to get cooler, leaves begin to change color, and crops are harvested.

In December, winter begins. Winter is the coldest time of year. Except for the evergreens, the trees are bare, and snow covers the ground in many parts of the country.

Summer Days

By Christina G. Rossetti

Winter is cold-hearted;
Spring is yea and nay;
Autumn is a weathercock;
Blown every way:
Summer days for me
When every leaf is on its tree,

When Robin's not a beggar,
And Jenny Wren's a bride,
And Larks hang, singing, singing, singing,
Over the wheat-fields wide,
And anchored lilies ride,

And the pendulum spider,
Swings from side to side,

And blue-black beetles transact business,
And gnats fly in a host,
And furry caterpillars hasten
That no time be lost,
And moths grow fat and thrive,
And lady birds arrive.

Before green apples blush,
Before green nuts embrown,
Why one day in the country
Is worth a month in town—
Is worth a day and a year
Of the dusty, musty, lag-last fashion
That days drone elsewhere.

The Fox and the Hedgehog

An Aesop's Fable

A Fox, swimming across a river, was barely able to reach the bank where he lay bruised and exhausted from his struggle with the swift current. Soon a swarm of blood-sucking flies settled on him; but he lay quietly, still too weak to run away from them.

A Hedgehog happened by. "Let me drive the flies away," he said kindly.

"No, no!" exclaimed the Fox. "Do not disturb them! They have taken all they can hold. If you drive them away, another greedy swarm will come and take the little blood I have left."

Better to bear a lesser evil than to risk a greater in removing it.

Copywork

Literature

"Have I kept my word?" said Mowgli.

Poetry—Summer Days

Winter is cold-hearted;

50. The Four Seasons

- The Jungle Book: The White Seal (first half)

The four seasons are winter, spring, summer, and fall.

Say the seasons three times today and every lesson day until you can recite them without help. Today's poem is about one of the seasons: spring! Many people love spring because it heralds the return of warmer weather and the rebirth of the land.

Spring
By William Blake

Sound the flute!
Now it's mute!
Birds delight,
Day and night,
Nightingale,
In the dale,
Lark in sky,—
Merrily,
Merrily, merrily to welcome in the year.

Little boy,
Full of joy;
Little girl,
Sweet and small;
Cock does crow,
So do you;
Merry voice,
Infant noise;
Merrily, merrily to welcome in the year.

Little lamb,
Here I am;
Come and lick

My white neck;
Let me pull
Your soft wool;
Let me kiss
Your soft face;
Merrily, merrily we welcome in the year.

The Bat and the Weasels

An Aesop's Fable

A Bat blundered into the nest of a Weasel, who ran up to catch and eat him. The Bat begged for his life, but the Weasel would not listen.

"You are a Mouse," he said, "and I am a sworn enemy of Mice. Every Mouse I catch, I am going to eat!"

"But I am not a Mouse!" cried the Bat. "Look at my wings. Can Mice fly? Why, I am only a Bird! Please let me go!"

The Weasel had to admit that the Bat was not a Mouse, so he let him go. But a few days later, the foolish Bat went blindly into the nest of another Weasel. This Weasel happened to be a bitter enemy of Birds, and he soon had the Bat under his claws, ready to eat him.

"You are a Bird," he said, "and I am going to eat you!"

"What," cried the Bat, "I, a Bird! Why, all Birds have feathers! I am nothing but a Mouse. 'Down with all Cats' is my motto!"

And so the Bat escaped with his life a second time.

Set your sails with the wind.

Copywork

Literature

"Look at me!"

Maxim

Think before you speak.

The Luncheon of the Boating Party by Pierre-Auguste Renoir

Picture Study

1. Read the title and the name of the artist. Study the picture for several minutes, then put the picture away.

2. Describe the picture.

3. Look at the picture again. Do you notice any details that you missed before? What do you like or dislike about this painting? Does it remind you of anything?

51. The Four Seasons; Picture Study: The Luncheon of the Boating Party

- The Jungle Book: The White Seal (second half), Lukannon

The four seasons are winter, spring, summer, and fall.

Say the seasons three times today. Remember, when you can say them without help, then you only have to recite them once each lesson day.

Today's poem is about fall, which is also called autumn. During fall, the leaves die and fall off the trees, but they change into beautiful red, orange, and yellow colors before they do. The weather is not as hot as summer. Fall is also harvest time, when farmers collect the grains, vegetables, and fruits that have been growing throughout the spring and summer months. That's why we celebrate Thanksgiving in the fall.

The City of Falling Leaves

By Amy Lowell

Leaves fall,
Brown leaves,
Yellow leaves streaked with brown.
They fall,
Flutter,
Fall again.
The brown leaves,
And the streaked yellow leaves,
Loosen on their branches
And drift slowly downwards.
One,
One, two, three,
One, two, five.
All Venice is a falling of autumn leaves—
Brown,
And yellow streaked with brown.

Copywork

Literature

"Look out for yourselves!"

52. The Four Seasons

- The Jungle Book: "Rikki-Tikki-Tavi" (first half)

The four seasons are winter, spring, summer, and fall.

Say the seasons three times today. Remember, when you can say them without help, then you only have to recite them once each lesson day.

Today's poem is about winter. Winter is the coldest time of year. The grass is dead and brown, the trees are bare. Depending upon where you live, you may have a little or a lot of snow. Some people love winter for winter sports like skiing and sledding and just playing in the snow.

Winter-Time

By Robert Louis Stevenson

Late lies the wintry sun a-bed,
A frosty, fiery sleepy-head;
Blinks but an hour or two; and then,
A blood-red orange, sets again.

Before the stars have left the skies,
At morning in the dark I rise;
And shivering in my nakedness,
By the cold candle, bathe and dress.

Close by the jolly fire I sit
To warm my frozen bones a bit;
Or with a reindeer-sled, explore
The colder countries round the door.

When to go out, my nurse doth wrap
Me in my comforter and cap;
The cold wind burns my face, and blows
Its frosty pepper up my nose.

Black are my steps on silver sod;
Thick blows my frosty breath abroad;
And tree and house, and hill and lake,
Are frosted like a wedding cake.

The Quack Toad

An Aesop's Fable

An old Toad once informed all his neighbors that he was a learned doctor. In fact, he could cure anything. The Fox heard the news and hurried to see the Toad. He looked the Toad over very carefully.

"Mr. Toad," he said, "I've been told that you cure anything! But just take a look at yourself, and then try some of your own medicine. If you can cure yourself of that blotchy skin and that rheumatic gait, someone might believe you. Otherwise, I should advise you to try some other profession."

Those who would mend others should first mend themselves.

Copywork

Literature

"What is the matter?" asked Rikki-tikki.

Poetry—Summer Days

Spring is yea and nay;

53. The Four Seasons

• The Jungle Book: "Rikki-Tikki-Tavi" (second half), Darzee's Chant

The four seasons are winter, spring, summer, and fall.

Can you say the seasons without help now?

Today's poem is mostly about summer. Summer is the hottest time of year. In summer, flowers are in bloom, grass is green, trees are full of leaves. Summer days are long, with daylight lasting until late in the evening.

Playgrounds

By Laurence Alma-Tadema

In summer I am very glad
We children are so small,
For we can see a thousand things
That men can't see at all.

They don't know much about the moss
And all the stones they pass:
They never lie and play among
The forests in the grass:

They walk about a long way off;
And, when we're at the sea,
Let father stoop as best he can
He can't find things like me.

But, when the snow is on the ground
And all the puddles freeze,
I wish that I were very tall,
High up above the trees.

The Fox Without a Tail

An Aesop's Fable

A Fox that had been caught in a trap succeeded at last, after much painful tugging, in getting away. But he had to leave his beautiful bushy tail behind him.

For a long time he kept away from the other Foxes, for he knew well enough that they would all make fun of him and crack jokes and laugh behind his back. But it was hard for him to live alone, and at last he thought of a plan that would perhaps help him out of his trouble.

He called a meeting of all the Foxes, saying that he had something of great importance to tell the tribe.

When they were all gathered together, the Fox Without a Tail got up and made a long speech about those Foxes who had come to harm because of their tails.

This one had been caught by hounds when his tail had become entangled in the hedge. That one had not been able to run fast enough because of the weight of his brush. Besides, it was well known, he said, that men hunt Foxes simply for their tails, which they cut off as prizes of the hunt. With such proof of the danger and uselessness of having a tail, said Master Fox, he would advise every Fox to cut it off, if he valued life and safety.

When he had finished talking, an old Fox arose and said, smiling, "Master Fox, kindly turn around for a moment, and you shall have your answer."

When the poor Fox Without a Tail turned around, there arose such a storm of jeers and hooting that he saw how useless it was to try any longer to persuade the Foxes to part with their tails.

Do not listen to the advice of him who seeks to lower you to his own level.

Copywork

Literature

But he did not grow too proud.

Maxim

Let sleeping dogs lie.

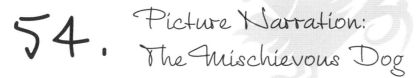

54. Picture Narration: The Mischievous Dog

- The Jungle Book: Toomai of the Elephants (first half)

The Mischievous Dog

An Aesop's Fable

There was once a Dog who was so ill-natured and mischievous that his Master had to fasten a heavy wooden clog about his neck to keep him from annoying visitors and neighbors. But the Dog seemed to be very proud of the clog and dragged it about noisily as if he wished to attract everybody's attention. He was not able to impress anyone.

"You would be wiser," said an old acquaintance, "to keep quietly out of sight with that clog. Do you want everybody to know what a disgraceful and ill-natured Dog you are?"

Notoriety is not fame.

Picture Narration

Draw a picture of the Aesop's fable from today. Show your picture to your instructor and tell her about it.

From a Railway Carriage

By Robert Louis Stevenson

Faster than fairies, faster than witches,
Bridges and houses, hedges and ditches;
And charging along like troops in a battle
All through the meadows the horses and cattle:
All of the sights of the hill and the plain
Fly as thick as driving rain;
And ever again, in the wink of an eye,
Painted stations whistle by.

Here is a child who clambers and scrambles,
All by himself and gathering brambles;
Here is a tramp who stands and gazes;
And here is the green for stringing the daisies!
Here is a cart run away in the road
Lumping along with man and load;
And here is a mill, and there is a river:
Each a glimpse and gone forever!

Copywork

Literature

"Yes," said Little Toomai, "he is afraid of me."

55. Introducing the Months of the Year

- The Jungle Book: Toomai of the Elephants (second half),
  Shiv and the Grasshopper

The months of the year are January, February, March, April, May,
June, July, August, September, October, November, and December.

You have a new list to start memorizing today! There are twelve months in the year.
The days of the week, the seasons of the year, and the months of the year are all ways
to help us keep track of time. Do you know the month in which you were born? We
call the month and the day on which you were born your birthday.

When Jenny Wren Was Young

A Mother Goose Rhyme

'Twas once upon a time, when Jenny Wren was young,
So daintily she danced and so prettily she sung,
Robin Redbreast lost his heart, for he was a gallant bird;
So he doffed his hat to Jenny Wren, requesting to be heard.

O, dearest Jenny Wren, if you will but be mine,
You shall feed on cherry-pie and drink new currant wine,
I'll dress you like a goldfinch or any peacock gay;
So, dearest Jen, if you'll be mine, let us appoint the day.

Jenny blushed behind her fan and thus declared her mind:
Since, dearest Bob, I love you well, I take your offer kind;
Cherry-pie is very nice and so is currant wine,
But I must wear my plain brown gown and never go too fine.

The Monkey and the Dolphin

An Aesop's Fable

It happened once upon a time that a certain Greek ship bound for Athens was wrecked off the coast close to Piraeus, the port of Athens. Had it not been for the Dolphins, who at that time were very friendly toward mankind and especially toward Athenians, all would have perished. But the Dolphins took the shipwrecked people on their backs and swam with them to shore.

Now it was the custom among the Greeks to take their pet monkeys and dogs with them whenever they went on a voyage. So when one of the Dolphins saw a Monkey struggling in the water, he thought it was a man and made the Monkey climb up on his back. Then off he swam with him toward the shore.

The Monkey sat up, grave and dignified, on the Dolphin's back.

"You are a citizen of illustrious Athens, are you not?" asked the Dolphin politely.

"Yes," answered the Monkey, proudly. "My family is one of the noblest in the city."

"Indeed," said the Dolphin. "Then of course you often visit Piraeus."

"Yes, yes," replied the Monkey. "Indeed, I do. I am with him constantly. Piraeus is my very best friend."

This answer took the Dolphin by surprise, and, turning his head, he now saw what it was he was carrying. Without more ado, he dived and left the foolish Monkey to take care of himself while he swam off in search of some human being to save.

One falsehood leads to another.

Copywork

Literature

"The child speaks truth," said he.

Poetry—Summer Days

Autumn is a weathercock;

56. The Months of the Year

- The Jungle Book: Her Majesty's Servants (first half)

The months of the year are January, February, March, April, May, June, July, August, September, October, November, and December.

Say the months of the year three times each lesson time until you have them memorized. Once you have them memorized, you need only recite them once. We always capitalize the names of the months.

The months of the years help us keep track of holidays! New Year's Day comes in January, St. Valentine's Day in February, St. Patrick's Day in March. October brings Halloween, November brings Thanksgiving, and December brings Christmas. What are your favorite holidays? In which month do they take place?

Snow-flakes

By Henry Wadsworth Longfellow

Out of the bosom of the Air,
Out of the cloud-folds of her garments shaken,
Over the woodlands brown and bare,
Over the harvest-fields forsaken,
Silent, and soft, and slow
Descends the snow.

Even as our cloudy fancies take
Suddenly shape in some divine expression,
Even as the troubled heart doth make
In the white countenance confession,
The troubled sky reveals
The grief it feels.

This is the poem of the air,
Slowly in silent syllables recorded;
This is the secret of despair,

Long in its cloudy bosom hoarded,
Now whispered and revealed
To wood and field.

The Rose and the Butterfly

An Aesop's Fable

A Butterfly once fell in love with a beautiful Rose. The Rose was not indifferent, for the Butterfly's wings were powdered in a charming pattern of gold and silver. And so, when he fluttered near and told how he loved her, she blushed rosily and said yes. After much pretty love-making and many whispered vows of constancy, the Butterfly took a tender leave of his sweetheart.

But alas! It was a long time before he came back to her.

"Is this your constancy?" she exclaimed tearfully. "It is ages since you went away, and all the time, you have been carrying on with all sorts of flowers. I saw you kiss Miss Geranium, and you fluttered around Miss Mignonette until Honey Bee chased you away. I wish he had stung you!"

"Constancy!" laughed the Butterfly. "I had no sooner left you than I saw Zephyr kissing you. You carried on scandalously with Mr. Bumble Bee, and you made eyes at every single Bug you could see. You can't expect any constancy from me!"

Do not expect constancy in others if you have none yourself.

Copywork

Literature

"It's too dark to see much."

Maxim

A stitch in time saves nine.

Ball at the Moulin de la Galette by Pierre Auguste Renoir

Picture Study

1. Read the title and the name of the artist. Study the picture for several minutes, then put the picture away.

2. Describe the picture.

3. Look at the picture again. Do you notice any details that you missed before? What do you like or dislike about this painting? Does it remind you of anything?

57. The Months of the Year

- The Jungle Book: Her Majesty's Servants (second half),
  Parade Song of the Camp Animals

The months of the year are January, February, March, April, May,
June, July, August, September, October, November, and December.

To March

By Emily Dickinson

Dear March, come in!
How glad I am!
I looked for you before.
Put down your hat
You must have walked
How out of breath you are!
Dear March, how are you?
And the rest?
Did you leave Nature well?
Oh, March, come right upstairs with me,
I have so much to tell!

I got your letter, and the birds';
The maples never knew
That you were coming, I declare,
How red their faces grew!
But, March, forgive me
And all those hills
You left for me to hue;
There was no purple suitable,
You took it all with you.

Who knocks? That April!
Lock the door!
I will not be pursued!
He stayed away a year, to call
When I am occupied.
But trifles look so trivial
As soon as you have come,
That blame is just as dear as praise
And praise as mere as blame.

Copywork

Literature

And the officer answered, "An order was given, and they obeyed."

58. The Months of the Year; Review

- Pinocchio by C. Collodi, Chapters 1-2

The months of the year are January, February, March, April, May, June, July, August, September, October, November, and December.

Say the months of the year three times each lesson time until you have them memorized. Once you have them memorized, you need only recite them once.

Let's review. Can you still say the seasons of the year and the days of the week without help?

Four Seasons

Anonymous

Spring is showery, flowery, bowery.
Summer is hoppy, choppy, poppy.
Autumn is wheezy, sneezy, freezy.
Winter is slippy, drippy, nippy.

The Cat and the Fox

An Aesop's Fable

Once a Cat and a Fox were traveling together. As they went along, picking up provisions on the way—a stray mouse here, a fat chicken there—they began an argument to while away the time between bites. And, as usually happens when comrades argue, the talk began to get personal.

"You think you are extremely clever, don't you?" said the Fox. "Do you pretend to know more than I? Why, I know a whole sackful of tricks!"

"Well," retorted the Cat, "I admit I know one trick only, but that one, let me tell you, is worth a thousand of yours!"

Just then, close by, they heard a hunter's horn and the yelping of a pack of hounds. In an instant the Cat was up a tree, hiding among the leaves.

"This is my trick," he called to the Fox. "Now let me see what yours are worth."

But the Fox had so many plans for escape he could not decide which one to try first. He dodged here and there with the hounds at his heels. He doubled on his tracks; he ran at top speed; he entered a dozen burrows—but all in vain. The hounds caught him and soon put an end to the boaster and all his tricks.

Common sense is always worth more than cunning.

Copywork

Literature

"Stop! You are tickling me all over!"

Poetry—Summer Days

Blown every way:

59. The Months of the Year; Punctuation Marks

• Pinocchio, Chapters 3-4

The months of the year are January, February, March, April, May, June, July, August, September, October, November, and December.

Can you say the months of the year without help? If not, say them three times today.

Remember that when someone asks a question in a story, the question mark is inside the quotation marks. Look at today's copywork from *Pinocchio* and name all the punctuation marks in the sentence.

"Tell me, Cricket, who may you be?"

Night

By Sara Teasdale

Stars over snow,
And in the west a planet
Swinging below a star—
Look for a lovely thing and you will find it.
It is not far—
It never will be far.

The Miser

An Aesop's Fable

A Miser had buried his gold in a secret place in his garden. Every day he went to the spot, dug up the treasure, and counted it piece by piece to make sure it was all there. He made so many trips that a Thief, who had been observing him, guessed what it was the Miser had hidden, and one night he quietly dug up the treasure and made off with it.

When the Miser discovered his loss, he was overcome with grief and despair. He groaned and cried and tore his hair.

A passerby heard his cries and asked what had happened.

"My gold! O my gold!" cried the Miser, wildly. "Someone has robbed me!"

"Your gold! There in that hole? Why did you put it there? Why did you not keep it in the house where you could easily get it when you had to buy things?"

"Buy!" screamed the Miser angrily. "Why, I never touched the gold. I couldn't think of spending any of it."

The stranger picked up a large stone and threw it into the hole.

"If that is the case," he said, "cover up that stone. It is worth just as much to you as the treasure you lost!"

A possession is worth no more than the use we make of it.

Copywork

Literature

"Tell me, Cricket, who may you be?"

Maxim

Curiosity killed the cat.

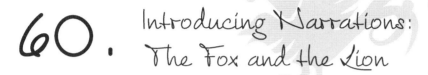

60. Introducing Narrations: The Fox and the Lion

- Pinocchio, Chapters 5-6

Today you will begin narration. You'll hear a very short Aesop's fable today, and afterwards, you'll tell the story to your instructor while she writes it down for you. Then you can draw a picture of the story!

[Note to instructor: Prompting is good. If the child has trouble, ask questions. What happened first? Then what happened?]

The Fox and the Lion

An Aesop's Fable

A very young Fox, who had never before seen a Lion, happened to meet one in the forest. A single look was enough to send the Fox off at top speed for the nearest hiding place.

The second time the Fox saw the Lion, he stopped behind a tree to look at him a moment before slinking away. But the third time, the Fox went boldly up to the Lion and, without turning a hair, said, "Hello, there, old top."

Familiarity breeds contempt.

Acquaintance with evil blinds us to its dangers.

A Book

By Emily Dickinson

He ate and drank the precious words,
His spirit grew robust;
He knew no more that he was poor,
Nor that his frame was dust.
He danced along the dingy days,
And this bequest of wings
Was but a book. What liberty
A loosened spirit brings!

"Would you be kind enough to give me a little bread?"

61. The Months of the Year

• Pinocchio, Chapters 7-8

Recite the months of the year, then read the poem "The Months" by Sara Coleridge. In this poem, she tells some of the things that we can expect in each month of the year.

The Months

By Sara Coleridge, adapted by Kathy Jo DeVore

January brings the snow,
Makes our feet and fingers glow.

February brings the rain,
Thaws the frozen lake again.

March brings breezes loud and shrill,
Stirs the dancing daffodil.

April brings the primrose sweet,
Scatters daisies at our feet.

May brings flocks of pretty lambs,
Skipping by their fleecy dams.

June brings tulips, lilies, roses,
Fills the children's hand with posies.

Hot July brings cooling showers,
Apricots and gilliflowers.

August brings the sheaves of corn,
Then the harvest home is borne.

Warm September brings fruit to eat,
Apples and melons and berries so sweet.

Fresh October brings the pheasants,
Then to gather nuts is pleasant.

Dull November brings the blast,
Then the leaves are whirling fast.

Chill December brings the sleet,
Blazing fire, and Christmas treat.

The Old Lion

An Aesop's Fable

A Lion had grown very old. His teeth were worn away. His limbs could no longer bear him, and the King of Beasts was very pitiful indeed as he lay gasping on the ground, about to die.

Where now his strength and his former graceful beauty?

Now a Boar spied him, and rushing at him, gored him with his yellow tusk. A Bull trampled him with his heavy hoofs. Even a contemptible Donkey let fly his heels and brayed his insults in the face of the Lion.

It is cowardly to attack the defenseless, though he be an enemy.

Copywork

Literature

"Open the door, I tell you!"

Poetry—Summer Days

Summer days for me

62. Review

- Pinocchio, Chapters 9-10

Let's review!

Can you name the vowels? When is **y** a vowel?

The vowels are **a, e, i, o, u**, and sometimes **y**. **Y** is a vowel when it sounds like a vowel. When it says /y/, it's acting as a consonant.

Can you name the days of the week?

The days of the week are Sunday, Monday, Tuesday, Wednesday, Thursday, Friday, and Saturday. What day of the week is it today?

Can you name the four seasons?

The four seasons are winter, spring, summer, and fall. Which is your favorite?

Can you name the months of the year?

The months of the year are January, February, March, April, May, June, July, August, September, October, November, and December. In which month were you born?

All But Blind

By Walter de la Mare

All but blind
In his cambered hole
Gropes for worms
The four-clawed Mole.

All but blind
In the evening sky
The hooded Bat
Twirls softly by.

All but blind
In the burning day
The Barn-Owl blunders
On her way.

And blind as are
These three to me,
So blind to someone
I must be.

The Donkey and the Grasshoppers

An Aesop's Fable

One day, as a Donkey was walking in the pasture, he found some Grasshoppers chirping merrily in a grassy corner of the field.

He listened with a great deal of admiration to the song of the Grasshoppers. It was such a joyful song that his pleasure-loving heart was filled with a wish to sing as they did.

"What is it?" he asked very respectfully, "that has given you such beautiful voices? Is there any special food you eat, or is it some divine nectar that makes you sing so wonderfully?"

"Yes," said the Grasshoppers, who were very fond of a joke. "It is the dew we drink! Try some and see."

So thereafter the Donkey would eat nothing and drink nothing but dew.

Naturally, the poor foolish Donkey soon died.

The laws of nature are unchangeable.

Copywork

Literature

He stopped and listened.

Maxim

April showers bring May flowers.

Girls at the Piano by Pierre Auguste Renoir

Picture Study

1. Read the title and the name of the artist. Study the picture for several minutes, then put the picture away.

2. Describe the picture.

3. Look at the picture again. Do you notice any details that you missed before? What do you like or dislike about this painting? Does it remind you of anything?

63. Introducing Nouns

• Pinocchio, Chapters 11-12

A noun is the name of a person, place, thing, or idea.

Today, you have a **definition** to begin memorizing. A definition is what a word means. We learn definitions when we're learning about a subject so that we can talk about a subject more easily. When we want to talk about words that name people, places, things, and ideas, it's easier to just say nouns! Say the definition of a noun three times each lesson until you have it memorized.

Everybody and everything has a name. We call those words nouns. A noun is the name a person, place, thing, or idea. We're going to start by looking at the first part of that definition: A noun is the name of a person.

You are a person. Are you a boy or a girl? **Boy** and **girl** are both nouns because they are names for people.

In your family, there are many kinds of people. You might have a **mother**, a **father**, a **grandmother**, and a **grandfather**. These words are all nouns that name people. Can you think of other nouns that name people in your family?

In *Pinocchio*, Pinocchio is a little marionette who lives with his father, Geppetto. Names for people are nouns. Since **Pinocchio, father**, and **Geppetto** are all names for people, they are all nouns. In the following sentence from *Pinocchio*, the names for people are underlined:

Think how poor <u>Harlequin</u> felt!

The Unseen Playmate

By Robert Louis Stevenson

When children are playing alone on the green,
In comes the playmate that never was seen.
When children are happy and lonely and good,
The Friend of the Children comes out of the wood.

Nobody heard him, and nobody saw,
His is a picture you never could draw,
But he's sure to be present, abroad or at home,
When children are happy and playing alone.

He lies in the laurels, he runs on the grass,
He sings when you tinkle the musical glass;
Whene'er you are happy and cannot tell why,
The Friend of the Children is sure to be by!

He loves to be little, he hates to be big,
'Tis he that inhabits the caves that you dig;
'Tis he when you play with your soldiers of tin
That sides with the Frenchmen and never can win.

'Tis he, when at night you go off to your bed,
Bids you go to sleep and not trouble your head;
For wherever they're lying, in cupboard or shelf,
'Tis he will take care of your playthings himself!

Copywork

Literature

"How do you come to know my name?" asked the puppet.

Exercise

Exercises can be done orally, or you can use the page in the optional workbook.

Find the nouns that name people in the following passage.

The next day Fire Eater called Pinocchio aside.

64. Nouns That Name People

- Pinocchio, Chapters 13-14

A noun is the name of a person, place, thing, or idea.

Say the definition of a noun three times each lesson until you have it memorized.

Think of the different people you have met. You know men and women, boys and girls. **Men**, **women**, **boys**, and **girls** are all nouns because these words name people. Besides your family, you might know a doctor whom you see when you are sick and a librarian who helps you find books. **Doctor** and **librarian** are both nouns because these words name people, too. Can you think of some other nouns that name people?

Pinocchio is a little marionette. **Marionette** is a common noun. A common noun is a noun that can be common to many people. Pinocchio is a little marionette, but so are many other characters in the story. But Pinocchio also has a special name all his own: Pinocchio! **Pinocchio** is a proper noun. When we talk about Pinocchio, we're not talking about just any little marionette, but one special little marionette. When we write someone's special, proper name, we begin it with a capital letter.

Look at this sentence from *Pinocchio*:

Fire Eater gives Pinocchio five gold pieces for his father, Geppetto.

Fire Eater, **Pinocchio**, and **Geppetto** are proper nouns because they name specific people. Geppetto is Pinocchio's father. **Father** is a common noun because there are many fathers. Pinocchio is a marionette. **Marionette** is also a common noun because there are many marionettes.

What is your special, proper name? What are the special, proper names for the people in your family?

Review

Name the punctuation marks in today's copywork from *Pinocchio*:

"Give ear to me, and go back, my boy."

Do you know what "give ear to me" means? He was telling Pinocchio to listen to him!

Under the Willow

By Leroy F. Jackson

Put down your pillow under the willow,
Hang up your hat in the sun,
And lie down to snooze as long as you choose,
For the plowing and sowing are done.

Pick up your pillow from under the willow,
And clamber out into the sun.
Get a fork and a rake for goodness' sake,
For the harvest time has begun.

The Heron

An Aesop's Fable

A Heron was walking sedately along the bank of a stream, his eyes on the clear water and his long neck and pointed bill ready to snap up a likely morsel for his breakfast. The clear water swarmed with fish, but Master Heron was hard to please that morning.

"No small fry for me," he said. "Such scanty fare is not fit for a Heron."

Now a fine young Perch swam near.

"No indeed," said the Heron. "I wouldn't even trouble to open my beak for anything like that!"

As the sun rose, the fish left the shallow water near the shore and swam below into the cool depths toward the middle. The Heron saw no more fish, and very glad was he at last to breakfast on a tiny Snail.

Do not be too hard to suit or you may have to be content with the worst or with nothing at all.

Copywork

Literature

"Give ear to me, and go back, my boy."

Poetry—Summer Days

When every leaf is on its tree.

Exercise

Exercises can be done orally, or you can use the page in the optional workbook.

Find the nouns that name people in the following passage. Which nouns are common and which are proper?

"Good morning, Pinocchio," said the fox.

"How do you know my name?" asked the marionette.

65. Nouns That Name Places

- Pinocchio, Chapters 15-16

A noun is the name of a person, place, thing, or idea.

Say the definition of a noun three times each lesson until you have it memorized. Nouns are the names for more than just people. The names of places are also nouns.

Do you like to go to the park or the zoo? Do you ever go to the store? **Park**, **zoo**, and **store** are all nouns that name places. These words are all common nouns because there are many parks, zoos, and stores. Each park, zoo, and store can also have its own special, proper name as well.

Think of some other places you like to go, or places you would like to go. Would you like to go see an ocean? **Ocean** is a common noun, but **Pacific Ocean** is a proper noun because it is the special, proper name of a specific ocean. Would you like to go to a mountain? **Mountain** is a common noun, but **Mount Fuji** is a proper noun because it is the name for a specific mountain. Would you like to go see a canyon? **Canyon** is a common noun, but **Grand Canyon** is a proper noun because it is the name of a specific canyon. Remember that proper nouns always begin with a capital letter.

Pinocchio sells his book to enter the marionette theater. **Theater** is a noun, too, because it is the name of a place. Is **theater** a common noun or a proper noun?

Theater is a common noun! There are many theaters. But the theater that Pinocchio goes to has a special, proper name, which is the **Great Marionette Theater**.

Think of some more places. Which names are common nouns and which names are proper nouns?

The Lily

By William Blake

The modest Rose puts forth a thorn,
The humble sheep a threat'ning horn:
While the Lily white shall in love delight,
Nor a thorn nor a threat stain her beauty bright.

The Fox and the Leopard

An Aesop's Fable

A Fox and a Leopard, resting lazily after a generous dinner, amused themselves by disputing about their good looks. The Leopard was very proud of his glossy, spotted coat and made disdainful remarks about the Fox, whose appearance, he declared, was quite ordinary.

The Fox prided himself on his fine bushy tail with its tip of white, but he was wise enough to see that he could not rival the Leopard in looks. Still he kept up a flow of sarcastic talk, just to exercise his wits and to have the fun of disputing. The Leopard was about to lose his temper when the Fox got up, yawning lazily.

"You may have a very smart coat," he said, "but you would be a great deal better off if you had a little more smartness inside your head and less on your ribs, the way I am. That's what I call real beauty."

A fine coat is not always an indication of an attractive mind.

Copywork

Literature

"You shall not escape from us again!"

Maxim

Virtue is its own reward.

Exercise

Exercises can be done orally, or you can use the page in the optional workbook.

Find the nouns that name places in the following passage. Which nouns are common and which are proper?

He saw a little cottage gleaming white as the snow among the trees of the forest.

66. Narration: The Wolf and the Sheep

- Pinocchio, Chapters 17-18

After listening to the Aesop's fable, tell the story to your instructor while she writes it down for you.

The Wolf and the Sheep

An Aesop's Fable

A Wolf had been hurt in a fight with a Bear. He was unable to move and could not satisfy his hunger and thirst. A Sheep passed by near his hiding place, and the Wolf called to him.

"Please fetch me a drink of water," he begged. "That might give me strength enough so I can get me some solid food."

"Solid food!" said the Sheep. "That means me, I suppose. If I should bring you a drink, it would only serve to wash me down your throat. Don't talk to me about a drink!"

A knave's hypocrisy is easily seen through.

The Little Turtle

By Vachel Lindsay

There was a little turtle.
He lived in a box.
He swam in a puddle.
He climbed on the rocks.

He snapped at a mosquito.
He snapped at a flea.
He snapped at a minnow.
And he snapped at me.

He caught the mosquito.
He caught the flea.

He caught the minnow.
But he didn't catch me.

Copywork

Literature

"My boy, you will repent it."

67. Quotations With Interrupting Speaker Tag

• Pinocchio, Chapters 19-20

Sometimes an author will say something right in the middle of a quotation! Look at the sentence below from *Pinocchio*. In the middle of the sentence, the author tells us who is speaking. When that happens, we need two commas to separate the quotation from the rest of the sentence. Point out the commas in the sentence.

> "What a good Fairy you are," said the puppet, "and how much I love you!"

Remember that a comma always follows a friend. When its friend is inside the quotation marks, so is the comma! And when the comma's friend is outside the quotation marks, the comma stays outside, too.

Your new poem to begin copying is called "Snow Song." Point out the capital letter that begins each line of the poem, and don't forget to capitalize the first letter when you're copying it!

Memory Work

The days of the week are Sunday, Monday, Tuesday, Wednesday, Thursday, Friday, and Saturday.

The four seasons are winter, spring, summer, and fall.

The months of the year are January, February, March, April, May, June, July, August, September, October, November, and December.

Snow Song

By Sara Teasdale

Fairy snow, fairy snow,
Blowing, blowing everywhere,
Would that I

Too, could fly
Lightly, lightly through the air.

The Wolf and the Goat

An Aesop's Fable

A hungry Wolf spied a Goat browsing at the top of a steep cliff where he could not possibly get at her.

"That is a very dangerous place for you," he called out, pretending to be very anxious about the Goat's safety. "What if you should fall! Please listen to me and come down! Here you can get all you want of the finest, tenderest grass in the country."

The Goat looked over the edge of the cliff.

"How very, very anxious you are about me," she said, "and how generous you are with your grass! But I know you! It's your own appetite you are thinking of, not mine!"

An invitation prompted by selfishness is not to be accepted.

Copywork

Literature

"What a good Fairy you are," said the puppet, "and how much I love you!"

Poetry—Snow Song

Fairy snow, fairy snow,

68. Nouns That Name Places

- Pinocchio, Chapters 21-22

A noun is the name of a person, place, thing, or idea.

Say the definition of a noun three times each lesson until you have it memorized.

Where do you live? Do you live in a town or a city? **Town** and **city** are names for places. They are common nouns because there are many towns and cities. Each town and city also has its own special, proper name, just like each child has his own special, proper name. What is the name of the town or city in which you live?

Your town or city is in a state, and the states are all in a country. **State** and **country** are common nouns; there are many states and countries. Our country is called the United States of America. **United States of America** is a proper noun since it is the special, proper name of our country. Our country has fifty states, and each has its own special, proper name, too.

Because they are proper nouns, the names of towns, cities, states, and countries always begin with capital letters.

Which state do you live in? Were you born in that state, or were you born in another state?

In *Pinocchio*, the story takes place in the country of **Italy**. That is where the author of Pinocchio lived! He was born in the city of **Florence**.

Can you think of other names for places?

The Rooks

By Jane Euphemia Browne

The rooks are building on the trees;
They build there every spring:
"Caw, caw," is all they say,
For none of them can sing.

They're up before the break of day,
And up till late at night;

For they must labour busily
As long as it is light.

And many a crooked stick they bring,
And many a slender twig,
And many a tuft of moss, until
Their nests are round and big.

"Caw, caw!" Oh, what a noise
They make in rainy weather!
Good children always speak by turns,
But rooks all talk together.

The Bear and the Bees

An Aesop's Fable

A Bear roaming the woods in search of berries happened on a fallen tree in which a swarm of Bees had stored their honey. The Bear began to nose around the log very carefully to find out if the Bees were at home. Just then one of the swarm came home from the clover field with a load of sweets. Guessing what the Bear was after, the Bee flew at him, stung him sharply, and then disappeared into the hollow log.

The Bear lost his temper in an instant and sprang upon the log tooth and claw to destroy the nest. But this only brought out the whole swarm. The poor Bear had to take to his heels, and he was able to save himself only by diving into a pool of water.

It is wiser to bear a single injury in silence than to provoke a thousand by flying into a rage.

Copywork

Literature

"I will never do it again."

Maxim

A penny saved is a penny earned.

Exercise

Exercises can be done orally, or you can use the page in the optional workbook.

Find the nouns that name places in the following passage. Which nouns are common and which are proper?

Pinocchio was awakened by sounds from the yard. He stuck his nose out of the doghouse.

The Fisherman by Pierre Auguste Renoir

Picture Study

1. Read the title and the name of the artist. Study the picture for several minutes, then put the picture away.

2. Describe the picture.

3. Look at the picture again. Do you notice any details that you missed before? What do you like or dislike about this painting? Does it remind you of anything?

69. Nouns That Name Things; Picture Study: The Fisherman

- Pinocchio, Chapters 23-24

A noun is the name of **a** person, place, thing, or idea.

Say the definition of a noun three times each lesson until you have it memorized.

So far, you've learned about nouns that name people and nouns that name places. Today, we're going to talk about nouns that name things.

Everything has a name, and those names are nouns. Look around the room you are in and name some of the things you see. Is there a **table**, a **couch**, a **bookshelf**? All of these words are common nouns.

Things can also have proper names. We've been reading a book. **Book** is a common noun that doesn't refer to any one, specific book. The book we've been reading is entitled *Pinocchio*. The title of a book is a special, proper name.

Your toys are all things. The word **toy** is a common noun because it can refer to many different things. Do any of your toys have a special, proper name?

When we talk about things, this can also include living things like plants and animals. The farmer who caught Pinocchio had a dog. **Dog** is a common noun, and the proper name of the farmer's dog was Melampo!

When Early March Seems Middle May

By James Whitcomb Riley

When country roads begin to thaw
In mottled spots of damp and dust,
And fences by the margin draw
   Along the frosty crust
Their graphic silhouettes, I say,
The Spring is coming round this way.

When morning-time is bright with sun
And keen with wind, and both confuse
The dancing, glancing eyes of one
   With tears that ooze and ooze

And nose-tips weep as well as they,
The Spring is coming round this way.

When suddenly some shadow-bird
Goes wavering beneath the gaze,
And through the hedge the moan is heard
    Of kine that fain would graze
In grasses new, I smile and say,
The Spring is coming round this way.

When knotted horse-tails are untied,
And teamsters whistle here and there,
And clumsy mitts are laid aside,
    And choppers' hands are bare,
And chips are thick where children play,
The Spring is coming round this way.

When through the twigs the farmer tramps,
And troughs are chunked beneath the trees,
And fragrant hints of s'gar-camps
    Astray in every breeze,
And early March seems middle-May,
The Spring is coming round this way.

When coughs are changed to laughs, and when
Our frowns melt into smiles of glee,
And all our blood thaws out again
    In streams of ecstasy,
And poets wreak their roundelay,
The Spring is coming round this way.

Copywork

Literature

"Oh, little Fairy, why did you die?"

Exercise

Exercises can be done orally, or you can use the page in the optional workbook.

Find the nouns that name things in the following passage. Which nouns are common and which are proper?

The jug was very heavy, and Pinocchio, not being strong enough to carry it with his hands, had to put it on his head.

70. Nouns That Name Ideas

- Pinocchio, Chapters 25-26

A noun is the name of a person, place, thing, or idea.

Say the definition of a noun three times each lesson until you have it memorized.

So far, you've learned about nouns that are the names of people, places, and things. People, places, and things all have a physical presence. They are real and solid. We can see, hear, smell, taste, or touch all of these.

The names of ideas are also nouns, but we can't reach out and touch ideas. We can't see, hear, taste, or smell them. But we can think about them and understand them.

Some ideas are our emotions, how we feel. Have you ever felt anger or sadness? **Anger** and **sadness** are both ideas, so their names are nouns. **Love** and **hope** can also be nouns. Can you think of others?

Not all ideas are about our emotions. Other ideas are **freedom**, **peace**, and **kindness**. Even though we can't see them or touch them, they're real and we can think about them.

The Fairy Forest

By Sara Teasdale

The fairy forest glimmered
Beneath an ivory moon,
The silver grasses shimmered
Against a fairy tune.

Beneath the silken silence
The crystal branches slept,
And dreaming through the dew-fall
The cold white blossoms wept.

The Dogs and the Hides

An Aesop's Fable

Some hungry Dogs saw a number of hides at the bottom of a stream where the Tanner had put them to soak. A fine hide makes an excellent meal for a hungry Dog, but the water was deep, and the Dogs could not reach the hides from the bank. So they held a council and decided that the very best thing to do was to drink up the river.

All fell to lapping up the water as fast as they could. But though they drank and drank until, one after another, all of them had burst with drinking, still, for all their effort, the water in the river remained as high as ever.

Do not try to do impossible things.

Copywork

Literature

"But you cannot grow," replied the Fairy.

Poetry—Snow Song

Blowing, blowing everywhere,

Exercise

Exercises can be done orally, or you can use the page in the optional workbook.

Find ALL of the nouns in the following passage. Can you find the two ideas? Which nouns are common and which are proper?

Pinocchio makes a promise to the fairy. His wish is to be a real boy.

71. Quotations With Interrupting Speaker Tags

- Pinocchio, Chapters 27-28

When the author tells us something about a quotation right in the middle of the quotation, we need two commas to separate the quotation from the rest of the sentence. Remember, commas always travel with the words they follow! If a comma follows a word that is inside the quotation marks, then it stays inside the quotation marks, too. If the comma follows a word that is outside the quotation marks, then it stays outside.

Find the commas in the sentence from *Pinocchio*. With which word is each comma traveling?

> "Really," said the puppet, "you make me inclined to laugh."

Historical Associations

By Robert Louis Stevenson

Dear Uncle Jim, this garden ground
That now you smoke your pipe around,
Has seen immortal actions done
And valiant battles lost and won.

Here we had best on tip-toe tread,
While I for safety march ahead,
For this is that enchanted ground
Where all who loiter slumber sound.

Here is the sea, here is the sand,
Here is simple Shepherd's Land,
Here are the fairy hollyhocks,
And there are Ali Baba's rocks.

But yonder, see! apart and high,
Frozen Siberia lies; where I,

With Robert Bruce and William Tell,
Was bound by an enchanter's spell.

The Rabbit, the Weasel, and the Cat

An Aesop's Fable

A Rabbit left his home one day for a dinner of clover. But he forgot to latch the door of his house, and while he was gone, a Weasel walked in and calmly made himself at home. When the Rabbit returned, there was the Weasel's nose sticking out of the Rabbit's own doorway, sniffing the fine air.

The Rabbit was quite angry—for a Rabbit—and requested the Weasel to move out. But the Weasel was perfectly content. He was settled down for good.

A wise old Cat heard the dispute and offered to settle it.

"Come close to me," said the Cat. "I am very deaf. Put your mouths close to my ears while you tell me the facts."

The unsuspecting pair did as they were told, and in an instant, the Cat had them both under her claws. No one could deny that the dispute had been definitely settled.

The strong are apt to settle questions to their own advantage.

Copywork

Literature

"Really," said the puppet, "you make me inclined to laugh."

Maxim

Better late than never.

Exercise

Exercises can be done orally, or you can use the page in the optional workbook.

Find all of the nouns in the following passage. Which nouns are common and which are proper?

"Open your eyes, Eugene! How shall I ever go home now? Why did I listen to those boys?"

72. Narration: The Dogs and the Fox

• Pinocchio, Chapters 29-30

    After listening to the Aesop's fable, tell the story to your instructor while she writes it down for you.

The Dogs and the Fox

An Aesop's Fable

    Some Dogs found the skin of a Lion and furiously began to tear it with their teeth. A Fox chanced to see them and laughed scornfully.

    "If that Lion had been alive," he said, "it would have been a very different story. He would have made you feel how much sharper his claws are than your teeth."

    It is easy and also contemptible to kick a man that is down.

The Ship of Rio

By Water de la Mare

There was a ship of Rio
   Sailed out into the blue,
And nine and ninety monkeys
   Were all her jovial crew.
From bo'sun to the cabin boy,
   From quarter to caboose,
There weren't a stitch of calico
   To breech 'em—tight or loose;
From spar to deck, from deck to keel,
   From barnacle to shroud,
There weren't one pair of reach-me-downs
   To all that jabbering crowd.
But wasn't it a gladsome sight,
   When roared the deep sea gales,
To see them reef her fore and aft
   A-swinging by their tails!

Oh, wasn't it a gladsome sight,
    When glassy calm did come,
To see them squatting tailor-wise
    Around a keg of rum!
Oh, wasn't it a gladsome sight,
    When in she sailed to land,
To see them all a-scampering skip
    For nuts across the sand!

Copywork

Literature

"Is the Fairy at home?" asked the puppet.

73.  Introducing Pronouns

- Pinocchio, Chapters 31-32

A pronoun is a word used in the place of a noun.

Today, you have a new definition! Say the definition of a pronoun three times each lesson until you have it memorized.

Look at these sentences:

> "Pinocchio can mount now, my boy," the little man then said to Pinocchio. "Have no fear. That donkey was worried about something, but the little man has spoken to the donkey and now the donkey seems quiet and reasonable."

That's how *Pinocchio* would read if we didn't have a special type of word called a pronoun. A pronoun is a word used in the place of a noun.

Say the definition of a pronoun three times each lesson until you have it memorized. We use pronouns because the sentences above are hard to say, hard to write, and hard to understand! See the difference when we put the pronouns back into these sentences:

> "You can mount now, my boy," he then said to Pinocchio. "Have no fear. That donkey was worried about something, but I have spoken to him and now he seems quiet and reasonable."

The underlined words are pronouns. Isn't that much better?
Now, look at this sentence from *Pinocchio*:

> "I intend to study, as all well conducted boys do."

Do you know what a "well conducted boy" is? He is a boy who behaves properly and follows the rules! Would you say Pinocchio has been a well conducted boy in the story so far?

The days of the week are Sunday, Monday, Tuesday,
Wednesday, Thursday, Friday, and Saturday.

The four seasons are winter, spring, summer, and fall.

The months of the year are January, February, March, April, May,
June, July, August, September, October, November, and December.

Written in March

By William Wordsworth

The cock is crowing,
The stream is flowing,
The small birds twitter,
The lake doth glitter,
The green field sleeps in the sun;
The oldest and youngest
Are at work with the strongest;
The cattle are grazing,
Their heads never raising;
There are forty feeding like one!

Like an army defeated
The snow hath retreated,
And now doth fare ill
On the top of the bare hill;
The ploughboy is whooping—anon—anon:
There's joy in the mountains;
There's life in the fountains;
Small clouds are sailing,
Blue sky prevailing;
The rain is over and gone!

Two Travelers and a Bear

An Aesop's Fable

Two Men were traveling in company through a forest when, all at once, a huge Bear crashed out of the brush near them.

One of the Men, thinking of his own safety, climbed a tree.

The other, unable to fight the savage beast alone, threw himself on the ground and lay still, as if he were dead. He had heard that a Bear will not touch a dead body.

It must have been true, for the Bear snuffed at the Man's head awhile and then, seeming to be satisfied that he was dead, walked away.

The Man in the tree climbed down.

"It looked just as if that Bear whispered in your ear," he said. "What did he tell you?"

"He said," answered the other, "that it was not at all wise to keep company with a fellow who would desert his friend in a moment of danger."

Misfortune is the test of true friendship.

Copywork

Literature

"I intend to study, as all well conducted boys do."

Poetry—Snow Song

Would that I

74. First Person Pronouns

• Pinocchio, Chapters 33-34

A pronoun is a word used in the place of a noun.

Say the definition of a pronoun three times each lesson until you have it memorized.

Do you know what the words singular and plural mean? **Singular** means only one, like the word **single**. **Plural** means more than one. We use different pronouns depending on whether the noun we're replacing is singular, only one, or plural, more than one.

First person pronouns are used when you speak about yourself. The first person singular pronouns are I, me, my, mine. Look at these sentences from *Pinocchio*. The first person singular pronouns are underlined.

"<u>I</u> recognized your voices immediately, and here <u>I</u> am."

"Hay gives <u>me</u> a headache!"

"Wait, <u>my</u> pretty Donkey."

"And today this good Fairy of <u>mine</u> sent a thousand fishes to the spot where I lay."

The first person plural pronouns are we, us, our, ours. In the following sentences from *Pinocchio*, the first person plural pronouns are underlined:

"<u>We</u> thank you for your attention!"

"Now show <u>us</u> how you can jump through the rings."

"Let us take off <u>our</u> caps together."

Five Little Chickens

A Traditional English Rhyme

Said the first little chicken,
With a strange little squirm,
"I wish I could find
A fat little worm."

Said the second little chicken,
With an odd little shrug,
"I wish I could find
A fat little bug."

Said the third little chicken,
With a sharp little squeal,
"I wish I could find
Some nice yellow meal."

Said the fourth little chicken,
With a sigh of grief,
"I wish I could find
A little green leaf."

Said the fifth little chicken,
With a faint little moan,
"I wish I could find
A wee gravel stone."

"Now see here," said the mother,
From the green garden patch,
"If you want any breakfast,
Just come here and SCRATCH!"

The Fox and the Goat

An Aesop's Fable

A Fox fell into a well, and though it was not very deep, he found that he could not get out again. After he had been in the well a long time, a thirsty Goat came by. The Goat thought the Fox had gone down to drink, and so he asked if the water was good.

"The finest in the whole country," said the crafty Fox. "Jump in and try it. There is more than enough for both of us."

The thirsty Goat immediately jumped in and began to drink. The Fox just as quickly jumped on the Goat's back and leaped from the tip of the Goat's horns out of the well.

The foolish Goat now saw what a plight he had got into and begged the Fox to help him out. But the Fox was already on his way to the woods.

"If you had as much sense as you have beard, old fellow," he said as he ran, "you would have been more cautious about finding a way to get out again before you jumped in."

Look before you leap.

Copywork

Literature

> And do you know what this sea-monster was?

Maxim

> Honesty is the best policy.

Exercise

Exercises can be done orally, or you can use the page in the optional workbook.

> Find the pronouns in the following passage. Which are singular and which are plural?
>
> > "I swear I shall never again taste fish."

Blind Man's Bluff by Jean-Honore Fragonard

Picture Study

1. Read the title and the name of the artist. Study the picture for several minutes, then put the picture away.

2. Describe the picture.

3. Look at the picture again. Do you notice any details that you missed before? What do you like or dislike about this painting? Does it remind you of anything?

75. First Person Pronouns; Picture Study: Blind Man's Bluff

• Pinocchio, Chapters 35-36

A pronoun is a word used in the place of a noun.

Say the definition of a pronoun three times each lesson until you have it memorized. Remember that first person pronouns are used when someone is speaking of himself, and singular means only one. The first person singular pronouns are I, me, my, mine. Complete each of the following sentences using a first person singular pronoun.

_____ made a marionette.

The marionette is for _____.

This is _____ marionette.

This marionette is _____.

Remember that plural means more than one. The first person plural pronouns are we, us, our, ours. Complete each of the following sentences using a first person plural pronoun.

_____ were swallowed by a shark.

The shark swallowed _____.

Tunny saw _____ escape.

My Kingdom

By Robert Louis Stevenson

Down by a shining water well
I found a very little dell,
    No higher than my head.
The heather and the gorse about
In summer bloom were coming out,
    Some yellow and some red.

I called the little pool a sea;
The little hills were big to me;
    For I am very small.
I made a boat, I made a town,
I searched the caverns up and down,
    And named them one and all.

And all about was mine, I said,
The little sparrows overhead,
    The little minnows too.
This was the world and I was king;
For me the bees came by to sing,
    For me the swallows flew.

I played there were no deeper seas,
Nor any wider plains than these,
    Nor other kings than me.
At last I heard my mother call
Out from the house at evenfall,
    To call me home to tea.

And I must rise and leave my dell,
And leave my dimpled water well,
    And leave my heather blooms.
Alas! and as my home I neared,
How very big my nurse appeared.
    How great and cool the rooms!

Copywork

Literature

    "Papa, help me, I am dying!"

Exercise

Exercises can be done orally, or you can use the page in the optional workbook.

Find the first person pronouns. Which are singular and which are plural?

"Lean on my arm, dear Father, and let us go. We will walk very, very slowly."

Find all of the nouns in the following passage. Which nouns are common and which are proper?

"The trap caught me and the Farmer put a collar on me and made me a watchdog."

76. *Second Person Pronouns*

• The Orange Fairy Book by Andrew Lang: The Ugly Duckling

A pronoun is a word used in the place of a noun.

Say the definition of a pronoun three times each lesson until you have it memorized.

Remember that First person pronouns are used when you speak about yourself. The first person pronouns are I, me, my, mine, we, us, our, ours.

Today, we shall learn about the second person pronouns. Second person pronouns are used for the person to whom we are speaking. The second person pronouns are you, your, yours. I might say to you:

> "How are <u>you</u> today?"

> "Is this <u>your</u> book?"

> "Are these toys <u>yours</u>?"

Look at this sentence from "The Ugly Duckling." The second person pronouns are underlined.

> "Can <u>you</u> ruffle <u>your</u> fur when <u>you</u> are angry or purr when <u>you</u> are pleased?"

Here, the cat is talking to the ugly duckling, so he uses the second person pronouns **you, your,** and **yours** to replace the duckling's name.

With the second person, the pronouns are the same for both singular, only one, and plural, more than one. In the following sentences from "The Ugly Duckling," the mother duck is talking to all of her children, but she uses the same pronouns that the cat used for just the ugly duckling!

> "<u>You</u> must go up and bow low before her," whispered the mother to her children, "and keep <u>your</u> legs well apart, as <u>you</u> see me do."

The Little Elf

By John Kendrick Bangs

I met a little Elf-man, once,
Down where the lilies blow.
I asked him why he was so small,
And why he didn't grow.
He slightly frowned, and with his eye
He looked me through and through.
"I'm quite as big for me," said he,
"As you are big for you."

The Porcupine and the Snakes

An Aesop's Fable

A Porcupine was looking for a good home. At last he found a little sheltered cave where lived a family of Snakes. He asked them to let him share the cave with them, and the Snakes kindly consented.

The Snakes soon wished they had not given him permission to stay. His sharp quills pricked them at every turn, and at last they politely asked him to leave.

"I am very well satisfied, thank you," said the Porcupine. "I intend to stay right here." And with that, he politely escorted the Snakes out of doors. And to save their skins, the Snakes had to look for another home.

Give a finger and lose a hand.

Copywork

Literature

"The new one is the best of all," said the children.

Poetry—Snow Song

Too, could fly

Exercise

Exercises can be done orally, or you can use the page in the optional workbook.

Find the first and second person pronouns. Which are singular and which are plural?

"Did you ever see anything quite as ugly as that great tall creature? He is a disgrace to any brood. I shall go and chase him out!"

77. Second Person Pronouns

• The Orange Fairy Book: The Enchanted Wreath

A pronoun is a word used in the place of a noun.

Say the definition of a pronoun three times each lesson until you have it memorized.

A pronoun replaces a noun in a sentence. When you are talking to someone, you use second person pronouns to replace that person's name.

The second person pronouns are **you**, **your**, **yours**. Whether we are talking to one person or to many people, we use the pronouns **you**, **your**, and **yours** to refer to the person or people we are talking to.

Complete each of the following sentences from "The Enchanted Wreath" using second person pronouns.

"Why do _____ sit there and get wet? Go and fly home to _____ nest."

"Besides, that daughter of _____ is a great strong girl."

Little Things

By Julia Fletcher Carney

Little drops of water,
Little grains of sand,
Make the mighty ocean
And the pleasant land.

So the little moments,
Humble though they be,
Make the mighty ages
Of eternity.

So our little errors
Lead the soul away
From the path of virtue,
Far in sin to stray.

Little deeds of kindness,
Little words of love,
Help to make earth happy
Like the heaven above.

The Lion and the Gnat

An Aesop's Fable

"Away with you, vile insect!" said a Lion angrily to a Gnat that was buzzing around his head. But the Gnat was not in the least disturbed.

"Do you think," he said spitefully to the Lion, "that I am afraid of you because they call you king?"

The next instant he flew at the Lion and stung him sharply on the nose. Mad with rage, the Lion struck fiercely at the Gnat but only succeeded in tearing himself with his claws. Again and again the Gnat stung the Lion, who now was roaring terribly. At last, worn out with rage and covered with wounds that his own teeth and claws had made, the Lion gave up the fight.

The Gnat buzzed away to tell the whole world about his victory, but instead he flew straight into a spider's web. And there, he who had defeated the King of beasts came to a miserable end, the prey of a little spider.

The least of our enemies is often the most to be feared.

Pride over a success should not throw us off our guard.

Copywork

Literature

"That is our secret," said the doves.

Maxim

Penny wise, pound foolish.

Exercise

Exercises can be done orally, or you can use the page in the optional workbook.

Find the first and second person pronouns. Which are singular and which are plural?

"I have dropped my axe in the forest. Bid your daughter go and fetch it, for mine has worked hard all day and is both wet and weary."

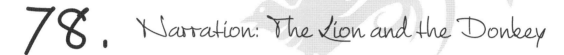

78. Narration: The Lion and the Donkey

- The Orange Fairy Book: The Clever Cat

After listening to the Aesop's fable, tell the story to your instructor while she writes it down for you.

The Lion and the Donkey

An Aesop's Fable

One day as the Lion walked proudly down a forest aisle, and the animals respectfully made way for him, a Donkey brayed a scornful remark as he passed.

The Lion felt a flash of anger. But when he turned his head and saw who had spoken, he walked quietly on. He would not honor the fool with even so much as a stroke of his claws.

Do not resent the remarks of a fool. Ignore them.

Song of Enchantment

By Walter de la Mare

A Song of Enchantment I sang me there,
In a green—green wood, by waters fair,
Just as the words came up to me
I sang it under the wildwood tree.

Widdershins turned I, singing it low,
Watching the wild birds come and go;
No cloud in the deep dark blue to be seen
Under the thick-thatched branches green.

Twilight came; silence came;
The planet of Evening's silver flame;
By darkening paths I wandered through
Thickets trembling with drops of dew.

But the music is lost and the words are gone
Of the song I sang as I sat alone,
Ages and ages have fallen on me —
On the wood and the pool and the elder tree.

Copywork

Literature

"Well, I must take the cat with me," answered the bird.

79. Third Person Pronouns

- The Orange Fairy Book: The Frog and the Lion Fairy

A pronoun is a word used in the place of a noun.

Say the definition of a pronoun three times each lesson until you have it memorized.

The first person pronouns are I, me, my, mine, we, us, our, ours. We use first person pronouns when we talk about ourselves.

The second person pronouns are you, your, yours. Second person pronouns take the place of the name of the person we are talking to.

Today, we will learn about third person pronouns. We use third person pronouns when we talk about everyone and everything else. The third person singular pronouns are **he**, **him**, **his**, **she**, **her**, **hers**, **it**, **its**. Remember that singular means only one.

We have a lot of third person singular pronouns! That's because we have pronouns for boys and men—he, him, his—pronouns for girls and women—she, her, hers—and pronouns for things—it, its.

Look at these sentences from "The Frog and the Lion Fairy." The third person singular pronouns are underlined.

The first thing <u>he</u> did was to plan how best to send <u>his</u> wife to a place of security.

<u>She</u> whipped up <u>her</u> horses till they ran away.

The castle was <u>hers</u>.

"Fix what ransom you like, for my husband will pay <u>it</u>, whatever <u>it</u> is."

Complete these sentences with a third person singular pronoun:

The Lion fairy was bored. _____ was bored.

She didn't hear from the king. She didn't hear from _____.

The King sent the queen away. _____ sent _____ away.

Memory Work

The days of the week are Sunday, Monday, Tuesday,
Wednesday, Thursday, Friday, and Saturday.

The four seasons are winter, spring, summer, and fall.

The months of the year are January, February, March, April, May,
June, July, August, September, October, November, and December.

At the Zoo

By William Makepeace Thackeray

First I saw the white bear, then I saw the black;
Then I saw the camel with a hump upon his back;
Then I saw the grey wolf, with mutton in his maw;
Then I saw the wombat waddle in the straw;
Then I saw the elephant a-waving of his trunk;
Then I saw the monkeys—mercy, how unpleasantly they smelt!

The Cat, the Rooster, and the Young Mouse

An Aesop's Fable

A very young Mouse, who had never seen anything of the world, almost came to grief the very first time he ventured out. And this is the story he told his mother about his adventures.

"I was strolling along very peaceably when, just as I turned the corner into the next yard, I saw two strange creatures. One of them had a very kind and gracious look, but the other was the most fearful monster you can imagine. You should have seen him.

"On top of his head and in front of his neck hung pieces of raw, red meat. He walked about restlessly, tearing up the ground with his toes and beating his arms savagely against his sides. The moment he caught sight of me he opened his pointed mouth as if to swallow me, and then he let out a piercing roar that frightened me almost to death."

Can you guess who it was that our young Mouse was trying to describe to his mother? It was nobody but the Barnyard Rooster, the first one the little Mouse had ever seen.

"If it had not been for that terrible monster," the Mouse went on, "I should have made the acquaintance of the pretty creature, who looked so good and gentle. He had thick, velvety fur, a meek face, and a look that was very modest, though his eyes were bright and shining. As he looked at me, he waved his fine long tail and smiled.

"I am sure he was just about to speak to me when the monster I have told you about let out a screaming yell, and I ran for my life."

"My son," said the Mother Mouse, "that gentle creature you saw was none other than the Cat. Under his kindly appearance, he bears a grudge against every one of us. The other was nothing but a bird who wouldn't harm you in the least. As for the Cat, he eats us. So be thankful, my child, that you escaped with your life, and, as long as you live, never judge people by their looks."

Do not trust alone to outward appearances.

Copywork

Literature

"I wish to see his Majesty," said he.

Poetry—Snow Song

Lightly, lightly through the air.

Exercise

Exercises can be done orally, or you can use the page in the optional workbook.

Find all of the pronouns in the following passage. Which are singular and which are plural?

"I am rich enough already," she answered, "but I am often dull, and I think you may amuse me a little."

Find all of the nouns in the following passage. Which nouns are common and which are proper?

Once upon a time there lived a king who was always at war with his neighbors.

80. Third Person Pronouns

• The Orange Fairy Book: The Princess Bella-Flor

A pronoun is a word used in the place of a noun.

Say the definition of a pronoun three times each lesson until you have it memorized.

Remember that plural means more than one. The third person plural pronouns are **they, them, their, theirs**. We use third person plural pronouns when we talk about more than one person or object.

We use the first person pronouns when we talk about ourselves: **I, me, my, mine, we, us, our, ours.**

We use the second person pronouns to replace the name of the person we are talking to: **you, your, yours.**

We use the third person pronouns to talk about others: he, him, his, she, her, hers, it, its, they, them, their, theirs.

Use third person pronouns to complete these sentences.

Once upon a time there lived a man who had two sons. _____ were his sons.

The older son left home. _____ left home.

The younger brother and his father stayed. _____ stayed.

The older brother inherited a box. The box was _____.

The stalls had the horses' names above them. The stalls had _____ names above them.

Butterfly

By Leroy F. Jackson

Butterfly, butterfly,
Sit on my chin,
Your wings are like tinsel,
So yellow and thin.

Butterfly, butterfly,
Give me a kiss;
If you give me a dozen
There's nothing amiss.

Butterfly, butterfly,
Off to the flowers,—
Wee, soulless sprite
Of the long summer hours.

The Flies and the Honey

An Aesop's Fable

A jar of honey was upset, and the sticky sweetness flowed out on the table. The sweet smell of the honey soon brought a large number of Flies buzzing around. They did not wait for an invitation. No, indeed; they settled right down, feet and all, to gorge themselves. The Flies were quickly smeared from head to foot with honey. Their wings stuck together. They could not pull their feet out of the sticky mass. And so they died, giving their lives for the sake of a taste of sweetness.

Be not greedy for a little passing pleasure. It may destroy you.

Copywork

Literature

"Take me," it said in a gentle whisper, "and all will go well."

Maxim

Charity begins at home.

Exercise

Exercises can be done orally, or you can use the page in the optional workbook.

Find the pronouns in the following passage. Which are singular and which are plural?

It was not until they were galloping breathlessly towards the palace that the princess knew that she was taken captive.

Education is All by Jean-Honore Fragonard

81. Introducing Verbs

- The Orange Fairy Book: The Bird of Truth

A verb is a word that shows action or state of being.

Say the definition of a verb three times each lesson until you have it memorized.

A noun is the name of name a person, place, thing, or idea. When we talk about nouns, we want to know what the person, place, thing, or idea is doing! A verb is a word that shows action. Verbs show what nouns do.

Can you think of some actions, things you like to do? Maybe you like to **run** and **play** outside. **Stand** up for a moment and **show** some action. Can you **hop**? **Skip**? **Jump**? Do you **read** this book, or do you **listen** while someone **reads** it to you?

Do you have brothers or sisters? What are they doing right now?

In "The Bird of Truth," one day, the fisherman **casts** his nets, and he **catches** two babies in his net! He **takes** them home. They **eat** and **drink** and **sleep** and **grow**.

All of the bold words are verbs. They express action and tell us what nouns are doing. If a word is something you can do, it is an action verb.

Memory Work

A noun is the name of a person, place, thing, or idea.

A pronoun is a word used in the place of a noun.

Picture-Books in Winter

By Robert Louis Stevenson

Summer fading, winter comes—
Frosty mornings, tingling thumbs,
Window robins, winter rooks,
And the picture story-books.

Water now is turned to stone
Nurse and I can walk upon;

Still we find the flowing brooks
In the picture story-books.

All the pretty things put by,
Wait upon the children's eye,
Sheep and shepherds, trees and crooks,
In the picture story-books.

We may see how all things are
Seas and cities, near and far,
And the flying fairies' looks,
In the picture story-books.

How am I to sing your praise,
Happy chimney-corner days,
Sitting safe in nursery nooks,
Reading picture story-books?

Copywork

Literature

"My good or evil fortune," replied the boy, "I know not which."

Exercise

Exercises can be done orally, or you can use the page in the optional workbook.

Find the action verbs in the following passage.

When they heard the story of the crystal cradle, they sat upright and looked at each other.

Find all of the nouns in the following passage. Which nouns are common and which are proper?

"And when the children are grown up, they can return to their father and set their mother free."

82. Verbs That Show Action

• The Orange Fairy Book: The White Slipper

A verb is a word that shows action or state of being.

Say the definition of a verb three times each lesson until you have it memorized.

A verb is a word that shows action. Can you **touch** your nose? Can you **walk** around the room? Can you **eat** your dinner? All of the bold words are action verbs. They tell us what you do. If you can do something, it is an action verb.

Usually, we can **observe** action verbs. I can **see** a bird **fly**. I can **hear** a dog **bark**. If a bug **touches** me, I can **feel** it. If something **burns**, I can **smell** it.

There are some action verbs that we can't observe. We can't see it when someone **thinks**, or when someone **knows** something, or when someone **dreams**. These are all still action verbs. We can do these things, but others can't observe the action. Can you think of any other invisible action verbs?

[Instructor: If necessary, prompt the child for invisible action verbs like hope, pray, love.]

Make sentences from the following nouns by supplying an action verb:

The baby _____.

The cat _____.

Cows _____.

My mother _____.

Birds _____.

Tigers _____.

Review

Look at your new poem to copy. Point out the capitalized first letter of every line, and remember to capitalize the first letter of each line in your copywork.

Rain

By Robert Louis Stevenson

The rain is raining all around,
It falls on field and tree,
It rains on the umbrellas here,
And on the ships at sea.

The Fox and the Monkey

An Aesop's Fable

At a great meeting of the Animals, who had gathered to elect a new ruler, the Monkey was asked to dance. This he did so well, with a thousand funny capers and grimaces, that the Animals were carried entirely off their feet with enthusiasm, and then and there, elected him their king.

The Fox did not vote for the Monkey and was much disgusted with the Animals for electing so unworthy a ruler.

One day he found a trap with a bit of meat in it. Hurrying to King Monkey, he told him he had found a rich treasure, which he had not touched because it belonged by right to his majesty the Monkey.

The greedy Monkey followed the Fox to the trap. As soon as he saw the meat, he grasped eagerly for it, only to find himself held fast in the trap. The Fox stood off and laughed.

"You pretend to be our king," he said, "and cannot even take care of yourself!"

Shortly after that, another election among the Animals was held.

The true leader proves himself by his qualities.

Copywork

Literature

"And you really think you can cure me?" asked the king.

Poetry—Rain

The rain is raining all around,

Exercise

Exercises can be done orally, or you can use the page in the optional workbook.

Find the action verbs in the following passage.

He snatched it from the case and thrust his foot into it, nearly weeping for joy when he found he could walk and run as easily as any beggar boy.

Find the pronouns in the following passage. Which are singular and which are plural?

And while he is on his way let us pause for a moment and tell who he is.

83. Review

- The Velveteen Rabbit by Margery Williams

It's time for another review!

Can you name the vowels? When is **y** a vowel?

The vowels are **a**, **e**, **i**, **o**, **u**, and sometimes **y**. **Y** is a vowel when it sounds like a vowel. When it says /y/, it's acting as a consonant.

Can you name the days of the week?

The days of the week are Sunday, Monday, Tuesday, Wednesday, Thursday, Friday, and Saturday. What day of the week is it today?

Can you name the four seasons?

The four seasons are winter, spring, summer, and fall.

Can you name the months of the year?

The months of the year are January, February, March, April, May, June, July, August, September, October, November, and December.

Now, look at your copywork sentence for today:

"Little Rabbit," she said, "<u>don't</u> you know who I am?"

Look at the underlined word. Do you remember what kind of word that is, and what the punctuation mark is called?

The word is called a contraction. A contraction is when we push two words together, and we make the word shorter by leaving some of the letters out. The punctuation mark is called an apostrophe. It takes the place of the missing letters. What two words make up the underlined contraction above?

Fly Away, Fly Away Over the Sea

By Christina G. Rossetti

Fly away, fly away over the sea,
Sun-loving swallow, for summer is done;
Come again, come again, come back to me,
Bringing the summer and bringing the sun.

The Mother and the Wolf

An Aesop's Fable

Early one morning a hungry Wolf was prowling around a cottage at the edge of a village when he heard a child crying in the house. Then he heard the Mother's voice say, "Hush, child, hush! Stop your crying, or I will give you to the Wolf!"

Surprised but delighted at the prospect of so delicious a meal, the Wolf settled down under an open window, expecting every moment to have the child handed out to him. But though the little one continued to fret, the Wolf waited all day in vain. Then, toward nightfall, he heard the Mother's voice again as she sat down near the window to sing and rock her baby to sleep.

"There, child, there! The Wolf shall not get you. No, no! Daddy is watching, and Daddy will kill him if he should come near!"

Just then the Father came within sight of the home, and the Wolf was barely able to save himself from the Dogs by a clever bit of running.

Do not believe everything you hear.

Copywork

Literature

"Little Rabbit," she said, "don't you know who I am?"

Maxim

Still waters run deep.

Exercise

Exercises can be done orally, or you can use the page in the optional workbook.

Find the action verbs in the following passage.

For a long time he lived in the toy cupboard or on the nursery floor, and no one thought very much about him.

Find all of the nouns in the following passage. Which nouns are common and which are proper?

The velveteen rabbit was naturally shy, and being only made of velveteen, some of the more expensive toys quite snubbed him.

84. Narration: The Two Goats

- The Box-Car Children by Gertrude Chandler Warner, Chapter 1

After listening to the Aesop's fable, tell the story to your instructor while she writes it down for you.

The Two Goats
An Aesop's Fable

Two Goats, frisking gaily on the rocky steeps of a mountain valley, chanced to meet, one on each side of a deep chasm through which poured a mighty mountain torrent. The trunk of a fallen tree formed the only means of crossing the chasm, and on this not even two squirrels could have passed each other in safety. The narrow path would have made the bravest tremble. Not so our Goats. Their pride would not permit either to stand aside for the other.

One set her foot on the log. The other did likewise. In the middle they met horn to horn. Neither would give way, and so they both fell to be swept away by the roaring torrent below.

It is better to yield than to come to misfortune through stubbornness.

Evening
By Emily Dickinson

The cricket sang,
And set the sun,
And workmen finished, one by one,
Their seam the day upon.

The low grass loaded with the dew,
The twilight stood as strangers do
With hat in hand, polite and new,
To stay as if, or go.

A vastness, as a neighbor, came,
A wisdom without face or name,
A peace, as hemispheres at home,
And so the night became.

Copywork

Literature

"Sh! Violet! Come!"

85.  Verbs That Show State of Being

• The Box-Car Children, Chapter 2

A verb is a word that shows action or state of being.

Say the definition of a verb three times each lesson until you have it memorized. We've already learned about verbs that express action. Today, we'll learn about verbs that show state of being. We'll start by learning a list of state of being verbs.

The state of being verbs are
am, are, is, was, were, be, being, been.

Say the list of state of being verbs three times each lesson until you have it memorized. State of being verbs do not show action, nor do they tell anything about someone or something. A state of being verb only says that someone or something exists.

I am.
You are.
He is.
She was.
They were.

State of being verbs can be used to answer questions, but they do not give any additional information. Use state of being verbs to complete these sentences.

Are you ready to complete this lesson? I _____.

Am I looking lovely today? You _____.

Is the kitten cute and furry? It _____.

Was the book fun to read? It _____.

Were the children playing? They _____.

Review

Look at the contraction in your copywork for today:

"What's the matter?" demanded Henry.

What two words were used to make this contraction? What is the punctuation mark in a contraction called?

What's is the contraction of **what is**, and the punctuation mark in a contraction is called an apostrophe.

Memory Work

The days of the week are Sunday, Monday, Tuesday, Wednesday, Thursday, Friday, and Saturday.

The four seasons are winter, spring, summer, and fall.

The months of the year are January, February, March, April, May, June, July, August, September, October, November, and December.

The Frog and the Centipede

Anonymous

A centipede was happy quite,
Until a frog in fun said:
"Pray tell which leg comes after which?"
This raised her mind to such a pitch,
She lay distracted in a ditch,
Considering how to run.

The Animals and the Plague

An Aesop's Fable

Once upon a time, a severe plague raged among the animals. Many died, and those who lived were so ill that they cared for neither food nor drink and dragged themselves about listlessly. No longer could a fat young hen tempt Master Fox to dinner, nor could a tender lamb rouse greedy Sir Wolf's appetite.

At last the Lion decided to call a council. When all the animals were gathered together he arose and said, "Dear friends, I believe the gods have sent this plague upon us as a punishment for our sins. Therefore, the most guilty one of us must be offered in sacrifice. Perhaps we may thus obtain forgiveness and cure for all.

"I will confess all my sins first. I admit that I have been very greedy and have devoured many sheep. They had done me no harm. I have eaten goats and bulls and stags. To tell the truth, I even ate up a shepherd now and then.

"Now, if I am the most guilty, I am ready to be sacrificed. But I think it best that each one confess his sins as I have done. Then we can decide in all justice who is the most guilty."

"Your majesty," said the Fox, "you are too good. Can it be a crime to eat sheep, such stupid mutton heads? No, no, your majesty. You have done them great honor by eating them up. And so far as shepherds are concerned, we all know they belong to that puny race that pretends to be our masters."

All the animals applauded the Fox loudly. Then, though the Tiger, the Bear, the Wolf, and all the savage beasts recited the most wicked deeds, all were excused and made to appear very saint-like and innocent.

It was now the Donkey's turn to confess.

"I remember," he said guiltily, "that one day as I was passing a field belonging to some priests, I was so tempted by the tender grass and my hunger that I could not resist nibbling a bit of it. I had no right to do it, I admit—"

A great uproar among the beasts interrupted him. Here was the culprit who had brought misfortune on all of them! What a horrible crime it was to eat grass that belonged to someone else! It was enough to hang anyone for, much more a Donkey.

Immediately they all fell upon him, the Wolf in the lead, and soon had made an end to him, sacrificing him to the gods then and there and without the formality of an altar.

The weak are made to suffer for the misdeeds of the powerful.

Copywork

Literature

"What's the matter?" demanded Henry.

Poetry—Rain

It falls on field and tree,

Exercise

Exercises can be done orally, or you can use the page in the optional workbook.

Find the action verbs in the following passage.

> She looked in every direction for shelter. She even walked quite a little way into the woods and down a hill. And there she stood, not knowing what to do next.

Find the pronouns in the following passage. Which are singular and which are plural?

> "I will get in, and you hand him up to me."

86. Introducing Abbreviations

- The Box-Car Children, Chapter 3

Do you know what the word abbreviation means? It means brief!

Sometimes when we write words, we use an abbreviation instead of writing the entire word. When we use abbreviations for the months, we only write the first three letters of the name of the month. Look at the abbreviations below. What is at the end of each abbreviation?

January	Jan.	July	Jul.
February	Feb.	August	Aug.
March	Mar.	September	Sep. or Sept.
April	Apr.	October	Oct.
May	May	November	Nov.
June	Jun.	December	Dec.

An abbreviation ends with a period.

The names of the months are proper nouns, so each abbreviation begins with a capital letter just as the name of the month does. Why doesn't the abbreviation for May end with a period?

Name all the punctuation marks in the sentence below. Can you point out the contraction? Which two words made up the contraction?

"I've found a place! Hurry! Hurry!"

Memory Work

A verb is a word that shows action or state of being.

The state of being verbs are
am, are, is, was, were, be, being, been.

Woodman, Spare That Tree

By George Pope Morris

Woodman, spare that tree!
　Touch not a single bough!
In youth it sheltered me,
　And I'll protect it now.
'Twas my forefather's hand
　That placed it near his cot;
There, woodman, let it stand,
　Thy axe shall harm it not!

That old familiar tree,
　Whose glory and renown
Are spread o'er land and sea,
　And wouldst thou hew it down?
Woodman, forbear thy stroke!
　Cut not its earth-bound ties;
O, spare that aged oak,
　Now towering to the skies!

When but an idle boy
　I sought its grateful shade;
In all their gushing joy
　Here, too, my sisters played.
My mother kissed me here;
　My father pressed my hand—
Forgive this foolish tear,
　But let that old oak stand!

My heart-strings round thee cling,
　Close as thy bark, old friend!
Here shall the wild-bird sing,
　And still thy branches bend.
Old tree! the storm still brave!
　And, woodman, leave the spot;
While I've a hand to save,
　Thy axe shall hurt it not.

The Oak and the Reeds

An Aesop's Fable

　A Giant Oak stood near a brook in which grew some slender Reeds. When the wind blew, the great Oak stood proudly upright with its hundred arms uplifted to the sky. But the Reeds bowed low in the wind and sang a sad and mournful song.

　"You have reason to complain," said the Oak. "The slightest breeze that ruffles the surface of the water makes you bow your heads, while I, the mighty Oak, stand upright and firm before the howling tempest."

"Do not worry about us," replied the Reeds. "The winds do not harm us. We bow before them, and so we do not break. You, in all your pride and strength, have so far resisted their blows. But the end is coming."

As the Reeds spoke, a great hurricane rushed out of the north. The Oak stood proudly and fought against the storm while the yielding Reeds bowed low. The wind redoubled in fury, and all at once the great tree fell, torn up by the roots, and lay among the pitying Reeds.

Better to yield when it is folly to resist than to resist stubbornly and be destroyed.

Copywork

Literature

"I've found a place! Hurry! Hurry!"

Maxim

We can do more good by being good than in any other way.

Exercise

Exercises can be done orally, or you can use the page in the optional workbook.

Find the action verbs in the following passage.

The dog lifted his eyes and wagged his tail feebly. He held up his front foot.

Find all of the nouns in the following passage. Which nouns are common and which are proper?

"Poor doggie," murmured Jess soothingly as she clambered out of the car.

The Music Lesson by Jean-Honore Fragonard

Picture Study

1. Read the title and the name of the artist. Study the picture for several minutes, then put the picture away.

2. Describe the picture.

3. Look at the picture again. Do you notice any details that you missed before? What do you like or dislike about this painting? Does it remind you of anything?

87. Verbs That Show State of Being; Picture Study: The Music Lesson

- The Box-Car Children, Chapter 4

A verb is a word that shows action or state of being.

The state of being verbs are
am, are, is, was, were, be, being, been.

Say the definition of a verb and the list of state of being verbs three times each lesson until you have them memorized.

State of being verbs do not show action, they only show that someone or something exists. Use state of being verbs to answer these questions:

Are you enjoying the book The Box-Car Children?
I _____.

Am I reading this lesson? You _____.

Were the children hungry? They _____.

Was Benny thirsty? He _____.

Review

First person pronouns replace the name of the person talking. The first person pronouns are I, me, my, mine, we, us, our, ours.

Second person pronouns replace the name of the person you are talking to. The second person pronouns are you, your, yours.

Third person pronouns replace the name of everyone and everything else. The third person pronouns are he, him, his, she, her, hers, it, its, they, them, their, theirs.

Use pronouns to complete these sentences:

Violet went ahead. _____ went ahead.

The four children slept on. _____ slept on.

It was the baker's voice! It was _____ voice!

The horse pulled the creaky wagon. The horse pulled _____.

A wagon was heard behind the children in the distance.
A wagon was heard behind _____.

The two girls stooped down to examine the obstruction.
_____ stooped down to examine _____.

Memory Work

A noun is the name of a person, place, thing, or idea.

A pronoun is a word used in the place of a noun.

Bird Song
By Laura E. Richards

The robin sings of willow-buds,
Of snowflakes on the green;
The bluebird sings of Mayflowers,
The crackling leaves between;
The veery has a thousand tales
To tell to girl and boy;
But the oriole, the oriole,
Sings, "Joy! joy! joy!"

The pewee calls his little mate,
Sweet Phoebe, gone astray,
The warbler sings,
"What fun, what fun,
To tilt upon the spray!"
The cuckoo has no song, but clucks,
Like any wooden toy;
But the oriole, the oriole,
Sings, "Joy! joy! joy!"

The grosbeak sings the rose's birth,
And paints her on his breast;
The sparrow sings of speckled eggs,
Soft brooded in the nest.
The wood-thrush sings of peace, "Sweet peace,
Sweet peace," without alloy;

230

But the oriole, the oriole,
Sings "Joy! joy! joy!"

Copywork

Literature

"I'm sorry we haven't cups," Jess remarked.

Exercise

Exercises can be done orally, or you can use the page in the optional workbook.

Find the action verbs in the following passage.

"Wet my handkerchief," Jess ordered briskly.

Find the pronouns in the following passage. Which are singular and which are plural?

But you should have seen him stare when he saw what she was holding!

88. Linking Verbs

• The Box-Car Children, Chapter 5

Today, you have a new list to begin learning. Say the definition of a verb and the list of linking verbs three times each lesson until you have them memorized.

A verb is a word that shows action or state of being.

The linking verbs are
am, are, is, was, were, be, being, been, become, seem.

Did you recognize the linking verbs? You should! Most of them are the state of being verbs that you've memorized!

Linking means to connect or join. Linking verbs connect a noun or a pronoun with more information about the person, place, thing, or idea.

State of being verbs only show that someone or something exists. They don't tell us anything else about the noun or pronoun. But we can also use them as linking verbs to say something interesting about the noun or pronoun.

Look at these sentences from *The Box-Car Children*:

She was the housekeeper.

If the book only said, "She was," that would not give us much information. Instead, it says that she was the housekeeper."

The bottles were cold.

If the book only said that the bottles were, that would not give us much information. Instead, it says that the bottles were cold.

"It is delicious."

Instead of just being told, "It is," we're told, "It is delicious."

Review

Name all the punctuation marks in the sentence below. Can you point out the contraction? Which two words made up the contraction?

233

"It's delicious!" declared Jess. "Cold as ice."

Buzzy Brown

By Leroy F. Jackson

Buzzy Brown came home from town
As crazy as a loon,
He wore a purple overcoat
And sang a Sunday tune.
Buzzy Brown came home from town
As proud as he could be,
He found three doughnuts and a bun
A-growing on a tree.

The Plane Tree

An Aesop's Fable

Two Travelers, walking in the noonday sun, sought the shade of a wide-spreading tree to rest. As they lay looking up among the pleasant leaves, they saw that it was a Plane Tree.

"How useless is the Plane!" said one of them. "It bears no fruit whatever and only serves to litter the ground with leaves."

"Ungrateful creatures!" said a voice from the Plane Tree. "You lie here in my cooling shade, and yet you say I am useless! Thus ungratefully, O Jupiter, do men receive their blessings!"

Our best blessings are often the least appreciated.

Copywork

Literature

"It's delicious!" declared Jess. "Cold as ice."

Poetry—Rain

It rains on the umbrellas here,

Exercise

Exercises can be done orally, or you can use the page in the optional workbook.

Find the linking verbs.

This was the strangest spot of all, for behind the little waterfall was a small quiet pool in which Jess had set the milk bottles the night before.

Find all of the nouns in the following passage. Which nouns are common and which are proper?

Milk suited Benny very well, however, so the older children allowed him to drink rather more than his share.

89. Linking Verbs

- The Box-Car Children, Chapter 6

A verb is a word that shows action or state of being.

The linking verbs are
am, are, is, was, were, be, being, been, become, seem.

Say the definition of a verb and the list of linking verbs three times each lesson until you have them memorized.

When we use state of being verbs, they just tell us that something exists. When we use linking verbs, we use them to connect a noun or a pronoun with more information about the person, place, thing, or idea. Look at these sentences from *The Box-Car Children*:

"You are a wonder!"

"It is a pretty watch."

"He was pretty hot," Henry went on.

Twelve ginger cookies were inside.

I'm going to give you a noun and a linking verb. Complete the sentence by saying something interesting about each noun.

You are _____.

Henry, Jess, Violet, and Benny are _____.

Their dog's name is _____.

The boxcar is _____.

The Wind

By Leroy F. Jackson

The wind came a-whooping, down Cranberry Hill
And stole an umbrella from, Mother Medill.
It picked up a paper on Patterson's place
And carried it clean to the Rockaby Race.
And what was more shocking and awful than that,
It blew the new feather off grandmother's hat.

The Cat and the Old Rat

An Aesop's Fable

There was once a Cat who was so watchful that a Mouse hardly dared show the tip of his whiskers for fear of being eaten alive. That Cat seemed to be everywhere at once with his claws all ready for a pounce. At last the Mice kept so closely to their dens that the Cat saw he would have to use his wits well to catch one. So one day he climbed up on a shelf and hung from it, head downward, as if he were dead, holding himself up by clinging to some ropes with one paw.

When the Mice peeped out and saw him in that position, they thought he had been hung up there in punishment for some misdeed. Very timidly at first, they stuck out their heads and sniffed about carefully. But as nothing stirred, all trooped joyfully out to celebrate the death of the Cat.

Just then the Cat let go his hold, and before the Mice recovered from their surprise, he had made an end of three or four.

Now the Mice kept more strictly at home than ever. But the Cat, who was still hungry for Mice, knew more tricks than one. Rolling himself in flour until he was covered completely, he lay down in the flour bin, with one eye open for the Mice.

Sure enough, the Mice soon began to come out. To the Cat, it was almost as if he already had a plump young Mouse under his claws. But an old Rat, who had had much experience with Cats and traps and had even lost a part of his tail to pay for it, sat up at a safe distance from a hole in the wall where he lived.

"Take care!" he cried. "That may be a heap of meal, but it looks to me very much like the Cat. Whatever it is, it is wisest to keep at a safe distance."

The wise do not let themselves be tricked a second time.

Copywork

Literature

"Well, why couldn't we, Henry?" struck in Jess.

Maxim

Once bitten, twice shy.

Exercise

Exercises can be done orally, or you can use the page in the optional workbook.

Find the verbs in the following passage. Which are linking verbs and which are action verbs?

"These are trick spoons," explained Henry.

Find the pronouns in the following passage. Which are singular and which are plural?

"I wonder if we couldn't fix up a regular swimming pool," he said.

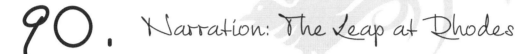

90. Narration: The Leap at Rhodes

- The Box-Car Children, Chapter 7

After listening to the Aesop's fable, tell the story to your instructor while she writes it down for you.

The Leap at Rhodes

An Aesop's Fable

A certain man who visited foreign lands could talk of little when he returned to his home except the wonderful adventures he had met with and the great deeds he had done abroad.

One of the feats he told about was a leap he had made in a city called Rhodes. That leap was so great, he said, that no other man could leap anywhere near the distance. A great many persons in Rhodes had seen him do it and would prove that what he told was true.

"No need of witnesses," said one of the hearers. "Suppose this city is Rhodes. Now show us how far you can jump."

Deeds count, not boasting words.

O Wind, Where Have You Been?

By Christina G. Rossetti

O wind, where have you been,
That you blow so sweet?
Among the violets
Which blossom at your feet.

The honeysuckle waits
For Summer and for heat.
But violets in the chilly Spring
Make the turf so sweet.

Copywork

Literature

"You just build it, and you'll see later."

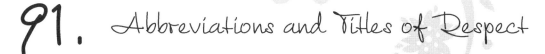

91. Abbreviations and Titles of Respect

• The Box-Car Children, Chapter 8

Remember that sometimes we use an abbreviation instead of writing out an entire word, like Jan. for January or St. for street. When we use the following titles of respect as part of a person's name, the title of respect is always abbreviated. Since these titles of respect are part of a person's name, they are capitalized.

Mister	Mr.	The title for a man.
Doctor	Dr.	The title for a doctor.
Mistress	Mrs.	The title for a married woman.

Although this abbreviation stands for "mistress," we actually pronounce Mrs. as "missuss."

The other two most common titles of respect are a little different. Miss doesn't have an abbreviation at all, and Ms. is only an abbreviation!

Miss	The title for an unmarried woman.
Ms.	This title may be used for either a married or an unmarried woman.

Memory Work

A verb is a word that shows action or state of being.

The linking verbs are
am, are, is, was, were, be, being, been, become, seem.

The Tide Rises

By Henry Wadsworth Longfellow

The tide rises, the tide falls,
The twilight darkens, the curlew calls;
Along the sea-sands damp and brown

The traveller hastens toward the town,
And the tide rises, the tide falls.

Darkness settles on roofs and walls,
But the sea, the sea in the darkness calls;
The little waves, with their soft, white hands,
Efface the footprints in the sands,
And the tide rises, the tide falls.

The morning breaks; the steeds in their stalls
Stamp and neigh, as the hostler calls;
The day returns, but nevermore
Returns the traveller to the shore,
And the tide rises, the tide falls.

The Donkey Carrying the Image

An Aesop's Fable

A sacred Image was being carried to the temple. It was mounted on a Donkey adorned with garlands and gorgeous trappings, and a grand procession of priests and pages followed it through the streets. As the Donkey walked along, the people bowed their heads reverently or fell on their knees, and the Donkey thought the honor was being paid to himself.

With his head full of this foolish idea, he became so puffed up with pride and vanity that he halted and started to bray loudly. But in the midst of his song, his driver guessed what the Donkey had got into his head and began to beat him unmercifully with a stick.

"Go along with you, you stupid Donkey," he cried. "The honor is not meant for you but for the image you are carrying."

Do not try to take the credit to yourself that is due to others.

Copywork

Literature

"You can actually swim a few strokes in it, Jess, if you're careful."

Poetry—Rain

And on the ships at sea.

Exercise

Exercises can be done orally, or you can use the page in the optional workbook.

Find the verbs in the following passage. Which are linking verbs and which are action verbs?

It was a hollow about three yards across. There were no stones in it at all.

Find all of the nouns in the following passage. Which nouns are common and which are proper?

The two older children dragged all the logs while Violet and Benny attended to the stones.

92. Introducing Adjectives

• The Box-Car Children, Chapter 9

A noun is the name of a person, place, thing, or idea.

An adjective is a word that modifies a noun or a pronoun.

Today you have a new definition! Say the definition of an adjective three times each lesson until you have it memorized.

Bird is a noun. If someone told you that he saw a bird, you might want to know more about the bird. Was it a large bird or a small bird? What color was it? Adjectives tell us more about nouns and pronouns by modifying, or describing, them. For now, we're going to talk about adjectives that describe nouns. Think about these words:

> soft, hard, funny, nice, short, tall, green, furry, cold, hot, wet, sweet, bitter, pretty, ugly

All of the above words are adjectives! We use them to tell us more about nouns. Can you think of a noun that could be described by each of the adjectives above?

Look at these sentences from *The Box-Car Children*:

> Henry, <u>slim</u>, <u>tanned</u>, and <u>graceful</u>, picked rapidly from the <u>tallest</u> ladder in the <u>largest</u> tree. The <u>two</u> girls leaned against the ladders easily about halfway up, their <u>fluffy</u> <u>short</u> hair gleaming in the sun. Benny trotted to and fro, waiting upon the <u>busy</u> pickers, his cheeks as <u>red</u> as the cherries themselves.

Slim, **tanned**, and **graceful** describe Henry. His tree was the **largest** and his ladder the **tallest**; **largest** and **tallest** describe the tree and the ladder. **Two** modifies the girls by telling us how many girls! Their hair is described as **short** and **fluffy**. All of the pickers are **busy**, and Benny's **cheeks** are as **red** as the cherries.

Nouns only name a person, place, thing, or idea. Adjectives describe the person, place, thing, or idea. They help us to picture exactly how the scene appeared.

Tit for Tat

By Christopher Morley

I often pass a gracious tree
   Whose name I can't identify,
But still I bow, in courtesy
   It waves a bough, in kind reply.

I do not know your name, O tree
   (Are you a hemlock or a pine?)
But why should that embarrass me?
   Quite probably you don't know mine.

The Farmer and the Cranes

An Aesop's Fable

Some Cranes saw a farmer plowing a large field. When the work of plowing was done, they patiently watched him sow the seed. It was their feast, they thought.

So, as soon as the Farmer had finished planting and had gone home, down they flew to the field and began to eat as fast as they could.

The Farmer, of course, knew the Cranes and their ways. He had had experience with such birds before. He soon returned to the field with a sling. But he did not bring any stones with him. He expected to scare the Cranes just by swinging the sling in the air and shouting loudly at them.

At first the Cranes flew away in great terror. But they soon began to see that none of them ever got hurt. They did not even hear the noise of stones whizzing through the air, and as for words, they would kill nobody. At last they paid no attention whatever to the Farmer.

The Farmer saw that he would have to take other measures. He wanted to save at least some of his grain. So he loaded his sling with stones and killed several of the Cranes. This had the effect the Farmer wanted, for from that day the Cranes visited his field no more.

Bluff and threatening words are of little value with rascals.

Bluff is no proof that hard fists are lacking.

Copywork

Literature

"What did it smell like?" inquired Benny.

Maxim

A good beginning makes a good ending.

Exercise

Exercises can be done orally, or you can use the page in the optional workbook.

Find the adjectives in the following passage.

> Even the merry little brook looked deserted.

Find the pronouns in the following passage. Which are singular and which are plural?

> "You see, this is a cherry year, and we have to work quickly when we once begin. Perhaps he could fill the small baskets from the big ones."

The See-Saw by Jean-Honore Fragonard

Picture Study

1. Read the title and the name of the artist. Study the picture for several minutes, then put the picture away.

2. Describe the picture.

3. Look at the picture again. Do you notice any details that you missed before? What do you like or dislike about this painting? Does it remind you of anything?

93. Introducing Possessive Nouns; Picture Study: The See-Saw

- The Box-Car Children, Chapter 10

Sometimes, we have things that belong just to us. When we want to show in our writing that something belongs to someone or something, we add an apostrophe and an **s** (**'s**) to the end of the noun. We call these **possessive nouns** because they show that a person, place, thing, or idea possesses, owns, or has something. The possessive nouns are underlined in the following sentences.

Benny rolled over on the grass and went to sleep with his head on the <u>dog's</u> back.

He liked the look of <u>Henry's</u> face.

<u>Jess's</u> family attacked the meal.

Review

A pronoun is a word used in the place of a noun.

Do you think we can replace possessive nouns with pronouns? We can! Some pronouns show possession. These are the possessive pronouns:

First person: my, mine, our, ours

Second person: your, yours

Third person: his, her, hers, its, their, theirs

Look at the sentences below. They're the same as the ones above, but the possessive nouns are missing. Which pronouns would replace the possessive nouns from the sentences above?

Benny rolled over on the grass and went to sleep with his head on _____ back.

He liked the look of _____ face.

_____ family attacked the meal.

Memory Work

The linking verbs are
am, are, is, was, were, be, being, been, become, seem.

An adjective is a word that modifies a noun or a pronoun.

Little Raindrops

By Jane Euphemia Browne

Oh, where do you come from,
You little drops of rain,
Pitter patter, pitter patter,
Down the window pane?

They won't let me walk,
And they won't let me play,
And they won't let me go
Out of doors at all today.

They put away my playthings
Because I broke them all,
And then they locked up all my bricks,
And took away my ball.

Tell me, little raindrops,
Is that the way you play,
Pitter patter, pitter patter,
All the rainy day?

They say I'm very naughty,
But I've nothing else to do
But sit here at the window;
I should like to play with you.

The little raindrops cannot speak,
But "pitter pitter pat"
Means, "We can play on this side,
Why can't you play on that?"

Copywork

Literature

"It's fun to run, anyhow," he thought.

Exercise

Exercises can be done orally, or you can use the page in the optional workbook.

Find the possessive noun. What pronoun could you use to replace it?

Henry was washing the concrete drives at Dr. McAllister's house.

Find the adjectives in the following passage.

The man tossed him a pair of white shoes and some blue trunks.

94. Adjectives That Tell How Many

• The Box-Car Children, Chapter 11

An adjective is a word that modifies a noun or a pronoun.

Say the definition of an adjective three times each lesson until you have it memorized.

Remember that a noun only names a person, place, thing, or idea. To modify or describe a person, place, thing, or idea, we need adjectives.

Many adjectives modify nouns by describing them. Adjectives can describe nouns by telling us about the color of nouns with words like **red, blue, light, dark,** and **bright**. Adjectives describe nouns by telling us about the **texture**, how something feels, with words like **smooth, spiny, rough, soft,** and **furry**. Adjectives can describe nouns by telling what we think about a noun with words like **ugly, beautiful, pleasant,** and **nasty**.

Adjectives can also modify nouns by answering the question **how many**. Numbers can be adjectives, but so can words like **few** and **many**. Look at these sentences from *The Box-Car Children*:

He had stopped at the Fair Grounds for a <u>few</u> minutes.

"I remember an old uncle of mine who put <u>two-hundred</u> dollars in the savings bank and forgot all about it."

In the first sentence above, **few** modifies **minutes** by telling us for how many minutes he stopped at the Fair Grounds. In the second sentence, **two-hundred** modifies **dollars** by telling us how much money the uncle had put into the bank.

The adjectives have been removed from this passage from *The Box-Car Children*:

He found a lunch waiting for him. Jess had boiled the vegetables in water, and the moment they were done she had drained off the water in a drainer and heaped them on the dish with butter on top.

And here is the passage with the adjectives put back into it:

He found a <u>delicious</u> lunch waiting for him. Jess had boiled the <u>little</u> vegetables in <u>clear</u> water, and the moment they were done she had drained off the water in a <u>remarkable</u> drainer and heaped them on the <u>biggest</u> dish with <u>melted</u> butter on top.

Now we know that lunch was **delicious** and the vegetables were **little**. We know that she used **clear** water instead of **dirty** water (yuck!) to cook the vegetables. We know that the drainer was **remarkable** and that she needed the **biggest** dish to hold them and the **melted** butter that she put on top.

Look around the room. Can you think of some adjectives to describe something you can see? Think about its size, shape, and color. How many adjectives can you think of to describe your favorite toy or your pet? Look outside and describe the weather.

Review

Remember to always capitalize the first letter in every line of a poem. Look at your new poem to copy and point out the capital letter that begins each line.

If You See a Tiny Fairy

By William Shakespeare

If you see a tiny fairy,
Lying fast asleep
Shut your eyes
And run away,
Do not stay to peek!
Do not tell
Or you'll break a fairy spell.

The Fighting Bulls and the Frog

An Aesop's Fable

Two Bulls were fighting furiously in a field, at one side of which was a marsh. An old Frog living in the marsh trembled as he watched the fierce battle.

"What are you afraid of?" asked a young Frog.

"Do you not see," replied the old Frog, "that the Bull who is beaten will be driven away from the good forage up there to the reeds of this marsh, and we shall all be trampled into the mud?"

It turned out as the Frog had said. The beaten Bull was driven to the marsh where his great hoofs crushed the Frogs to death.

When the great fall out, the weak must suffer for it.

Copywork

Literature

"Don't you see, Benny?" Jess explained patiently.

Poetry—If You See a Tiny Fairy

If you see a tiny fairy,

Exercise

Exercises can be done orally, or you can use the page in the optional workbook.

Find the adjectives in the following passage.

"He left it for over forty years, you see."

Find the possessive noun. What pronoun could you use to replace it?

Henry always insisted that the rat's tail was too long.

95. Introducing Articles

- The Box-Car Children, Chapter 12

The articles are a, an, the.

The articles—**a**, **an**, **the**—are three little words that you use so often with nouns, you probably don't even notice that you're saying them! Articles are adjectives because we use them to modify nouns. They don't describe nouns. Instead, they point out nouns.

The is a definite article because it is used to point out a specific noun. **A** and **an** are indefinite articles because they are used to point out any noun, not a specific noun. If your mother says, "Set **the** table, please," you know that she means a specific table: the dining table! If she ever says, "Set **a** table, please," you can set the coffee table instead!

Do you know why we have two indefinite articles? We use the article **an** before words that begin with vowels, and we use the article **a** before words that begin with consonants. Can you list the vowels?

The vowels are **a, e, i, o, u**. All other letters are consonants. So, to use an indefinite article with the word **apple**, we would say **an apple**.

Let's practice that. Answer the following questions with a noun, and use either **a** or **an** to modify the noun.

What type of citrus fruit is yellow and sour?

What is your favorite type of toy?

Where is your favorite place to go?

What sea creature has eight arms?

Memory Work

An adjective is a word that modifies a noun or a pronoun.

Name all the punctuation marks in the sentence below. Can you point out the contraction? Which two words make up the contraction?

> "Ginseng?" echoed Benny, thinking deeply. "That's a nice name."

That's is the contraction of **that is**, and the punctuation mark in a contraction is called an apostrophe.

A Candle, A Candle

By Leroy F. Jackson

A candle, a candle
To light me to bed;
A pillow, a pillow
To tuck up my head.
The moon is as sleepy as sleepy can be,
The stars are all pointing their fingers at me,
And Missus Hop-Robin, way up in her nest,
Is rocking her tired little babies to rest.
So give me a blanket
To tuck up my toes,
And a little soft pillow
To snuggle my nose.

The Goose and the Golden Egg

An Aesop's Fable

There was once a Countryman who possessed the most wonderful Goose you can imagine, for every day when he visited the nest, the Goose had laid a beautiful, glittering, golden egg.

The Countryman took the eggs to market and soon began to get rich. But it was not long before he grew impatient with the Goose because she gave him only a single golden egg a day. He was not getting rich fast enough.

Then one day, after he had finished counting his money, the idea came to him that he could get all the golden eggs at once by killing the Goose and cutting it open. But when the deed was done, not a single golden egg did he find, and his precious Goose was dead.

Those who have plenty want more and so lose all they have.

Copywork

Literature

"Ginseng?" echoed Benny, thinking deeply. "That's a nice name."

Maxim

The early bird catches the worm.

Exercise

Exercises can be done orally, or you can use the page in the optional workbook.

Find the articles. Does the word which follows **a** or **an** begin with a vowel or consonant? What other adjectives can you find in this sentence?

It was about a foot high with branching leaves and a fine feathery white flower.

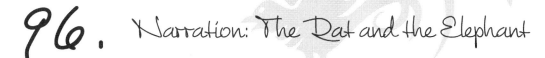

96. Narration: The Rat and the Elephant

• The Box-Car Children, Chapter 13

After listening to the Aesop's fable, tell the story to your instructor while she writes it down for you.

The Rat and the Elephant

An Aesop's Fable

A Rat was traveling along the King's highway. He was a very proud Rat, considering his small size and the bad reputation all Rats have. As Mr. Rat walked along—he kept mostly to the ditch—he noticed a great commotion up the road, and soon a grand procession came in view. It was the King and his retinue.

The King rode on a huge Elephant adorned with the most gorgeous trappings. With the King in his luxurious howdah were the royal Dog and Cat. A great crowd of people followed the procession. They were so taken up with admiration of the Elephant that the Rat was not noticed. His pride was hurt.

"What fools!" he cried. "Look at me, and you will soon forget that clumsy Elephant! Is it his great size that makes your eyes pop out? Or is it his wrinkled hide? Why, I have eyes and ears and as many legs as he! I am of just as much importance, and—"

But just then the royal Cat spied him, and the next instant, the Rat knew he was not quite so important as an Elephant.

A resemblance to the great in some things does not make us great.

Medusa

By Oliver Herford

How did Medusa do her hair?
The question fills me with despair.
It must have caused her sore distress
That head of curling snakes to dress.
Whenever after endless toil
She coaxed it finally to coil,
The music of a Passing Band

Would cause each separate hair to stand
On end and sway and writhe and spit,—
She couldn't "do a thing with it."
And, being woman and aware
Of such disaster to her hair,
What could she do but petrify
All whom she met, with freezing eye?

Copywork

Literature

One day Jess began to teach Benny a little arithmetic.

97. Possessive Nouns and Pronouns

• The Box-Car Children, Chapter 14

Possessive nouns and pronouns show that something belongs to a person, place, thing, or idea.

James Henry Cordyce's chauffeur was sent.

Mrs. McAllister had given the children's names clearly.

She had not added the man's name.

He went to sleep in the easy-chair in the doctor's big office.

Make a sentence about something that belongs to someone. Use a possessive noun in your sentence.

Complete these sentences with a possessive pronoun:

This is _____ toy.

The box-car is the _____.

Henry is _____ brother.

Memory Work

The days of the week are Sunday, Monday, Tuesday, Wednesday, Thursday, Friday, and Saturday.

The four seasons are winter, spring, summer, and fall.

The months of the year are January, February, March, April, May, June, July, August, September, October, November, and December.

In April's Sweet Month

A Mother Goose Rhyme

In April's sweet month,
When the leaves 'gin to spring,
Little lambs skip like fairies
And birds build and sing.

The Owl and the Grasshopper

An Aesop's Fable

The Owl always takes her sleep during the day. Then after sundown, when the rosy light fades from the sky and the shadows rise slowly through the wood, out she comes ruffling and blinking from the old hollow tree. Now her weird "hoo-hoo-hoo-oo-oo" echoes through the quiet wood, and she begins her hunt for the bugs and beetles, frogs and mice she likes so well to eat.

Now there was a certain old Owl who had become very cross and hard to please as she grew older, especially if anything disturbed her daily slumbers. One warm summer afternoon as she dozed away in her den in the old oak tree, a Grasshopper nearby began a joyous but very raspy song. Out popped the old Owl's head from the opening in the tree that served her both for door and for window.

"Get away from here, sir," she said to the Grasshopper. "Have you no manners? You should at least respect my age and leave me to sleep in quiet!"

But the Grasshopper answered saucily that he had as much right to his place in the sun as the Owl had to her place in the old oak. Then he struck up a louder and still more rasping tune.

The wise old Owl knew quite well that it would do no good to argue with the Grasshopper, nor with anybody else for that matter. Besides, her eyes were not sharp enough by day to permit her to punish the Grasshopper as he deserved. So she laid aside all hard words and spoke very kindly to him.

"Well, sir," she said, "if I must stay awake, I am going to settle right down to enjoy your singing. Now that I think of it, I have a wonderful wine here, sent me from Olympus, of which I am told Apollo drinks before he sings to the high gods. Please come up and taste this delicious drink with me. I know it will make you sing like Apollo himself."

The foolish Grasshopper was taken in by the Owl's flattering words. Up he jumped to the Owl's den, but as soon as he was near enough that the old Owl could see him clearly, she pounced upon him and ate him up.

Flattery is not a proof of true admiration.

Do not let flattery throw you off your guard against an enemy.

Copywork

Literature

"Couldn't I see them?" begged the man, almost like a boy.

Poetry—If You See a Tiny Fairy

Lying fast asleep
Shut your eyes

Exercise

Exercises can be done orally, or you can use the page in the optional workbook.

Find the possessive nouns. What pronoun could you use to replace each of them?

But something in the man's last sentence rang in Henry's ears.

98. Introducing Declarative Sentences

• The Box-Car Children, Chapter 15

A sentence begins with a capital letter and ends with a punctuation mark, and it must express a complete thought. Any group of words can begin with a capital letter and end with a punctuation mark, but if it doesn't express a complete thought, it is only a fragment. Fragment means a piece, so a fragment is only a piece of a sentence. Look at these examples:

The birds swooped and soared.

The birds.

The first is a sentence. It expresses a complete thought by telling us what the birds did. The second is only a fragment.

Look at these examples. Can you tell the fragment from the sentence?

Flying purple people eaters descended upon the city.

Descended upon the city.

The first is a sentence because it expresses a complete thought. The second is only a fragment.

There are four types of sentences, and we're going to talk about **declarative sentences** first.

A declarative sentence makes a statement. Its purpose
is to give information, and it ends with a period.

The following sentences from *The Box-Car Children* are statements, or declarative sentences. Notice how each one begins with a capital letter and ends with a period. Statements always end with a period.

In less than an hour the town was buzzing with the news.

But her grandfather did not seem to mind.

"And I noticed that he didn't tell much about himself, so I was curious."

Mr. Cordyce took note of this.

To Any Reader
By Robert Louis Stevenson

As from the house your mother sees
You playing round the garden trees,
So you may see, if you will look
Through the windows of this book,
Another child, far, far away,
And in another garden, play.
But do not think you can at all,
By knocking on the window, call
That child to hear you. He intent
Is all on his play-business bent.
He does not hear, he will not look,
Nor yet be lured out of this book.
For, long ago, the truth to say,
He has grown up and gone away,
And it is but a child of air
That lingers in the garden there.

The Donkey, the Fox, and the Lion
An Aesop's Fable

A Donkey and a Fox had become close comrades and were constantly in each other's company. While the Donkey cropped a fresh bit of greens, the Fox would devour a chicken from the neighboring farmyard or a bit of cheese filched from the dairy. One day the pair unexpectedly met a Lion. The Donkey was very much frightened, but the Fox calmed his fears.

"I will talk to him," he said.

So the Fox walked boldly up to the Lion.

"Your highness," he said in an undertone, so the Donkey could not hear him, "I've got a fine scheme in my head. If you promise not to hurt me, I will lead that foolish creature yonder into a pit where he can't get out, and you can feast at your pleasure."

The Lion agreed and the Fox returned to the Donkey.

"I made him promise not to hurt us," said the Fox. "But come, I know a good place to hide till he is gone."

So the Fox led the Donkey into a deep pit. But when the Lion saw that the Donkey was his for the taking, he first of all struck down the traitor Fox.

Traitors may expect treachery.

Copywork

Literature

"I didn't know, Benny," said Jess, turning pink.

Maxim

An apple a day keeps the doctor away.

Exercise

Exercises can be done orally, or you can use the page in the optional workbook.

Find the adjectives in the following passage.

"I hid behind the big white rock with the flat top."

Find the verbs in the following passage. Which are linking verbs and which are action verbs?

But her grandfather did not seem to mind.

They ate chicken sandwiches on the very same tablecloth, and Benny drank from his pink cup.

The Shepherdess by Jean-Honore Fragonard

Picture Study

1. Read the title and the name of the artist. Study the picture for several minutes, then put the picture away.

2. Describe the picture.

3. Look at the picture again. Do you notice any details that you missed before? What do you like or dislike about this painting? Does it remind you of anything?

99. Introducing Interrogative Sentences; Picture Study: The Shepherdess

- The Box-Car Children, Chapter 16

A sentence begins with a capital letter and ends with a punctuation mark, and it must express a complete thought. Look at these groups of words. Which is a sentence?

Chuckled to himself.

"You're going to school as soon as it begins."

The first group of words is not a sentence! It is a fragment because it does not express a complete thought. It does not tell us who chuckled to himself. The second group of words is a sentence because it does express a complete thought.

There are four types of sentences. You've already learned that a declarative sentence makes a statement. Its purpose is to give information, and it ends with a period. Today, you will learn about **interrogative sentences**.

Do you know what the word **interrogate** means? Police may interrogate a person suspected of committing a crime. Your mom may interrogate you and your siblings about who forgot to close the door. **Interrogate** means to ask questions. Now, can you guess what an interrogative sentence does?

An interrogative sentence asks a question! It ends with a question mark. Here are some questions asked in *The Box-Car Children*. Notice how each question, or interrogative sentence, begins with a capital letter and ends with a question mark.

"Do you live all alone, Grandfather?"

"Do you live here?"

"Can I run the cars all day?"

We can change each of these questions to statements, or declarative sentences! To do this, we have to rearrange the words a little, and each declarative sentence must end in a period.

Grandfather, you do live all alone.

You do live here.

I can run the cars all day.

Memory Work

A noun is the name of a person, place, thing, or idea.

A pronoun is a word used in the place of a noun.

Baby Seed Song
By Edith Nesbit

Little brown brother, oh! little brown brother,
Are you awake in the dark?
Here we lie cosily, close to each other:
Hark to the song of the lark
"Waken!" the lark says, "waken and dress you;
Put on your green coats and gay,
Blue sky will shine on you, sunshine caress you
Waken! 'tis morning 'tis May!"
Little brown brother, oh! little brown brother,
What kind of a flower will you be?
I'll be a poppy all white, like my mother;
Do be a poppy like me.
What! You're a sunflower! How I shall miss you
When you're grown golden and high!
But I shall send all the bees up to kiss you;
Little brown brother, good-bye.

Copywork

Literature

"Do you live all alone, Grandfather?" asked Benny.

Exercise

Exercises can be done orally, or you can use the page in the optional workbook.

Find the verbs in the following passage. Which are linking verbs and which are action verbs?

"He is the dog, all right. He knows me, as you see. His name is Rough No. 3. He has a black spot inside his ear."

Find all of the nouns in the following passage. Which nouns are common and which are proper?

The big car purred along from Greenfield to Townsend in no time.

100. Introducing Exclamatory Sentences

• The Box-Car Children, Chapter 17

A sentence begins with a capital letter and ends with a punctuation mark, and it must express a complete thought. Look at these groups of words. Which is a sentence?

> "O Grandfather."

> "I think I shall have to surprise you children."

The first group of words is not a sentence! It is a fragment because it does not express a complete thought. It does not tell us anything about Grandfather. The second group of words is a sentence because it does express a complete thought.

There are four types of sentences, and you've learned about two:

- A declarative sentence makes a statement. Its purpose is to give information, and it ends with a period.

- An interrogative sentence asks a question. It ends with a question mark.

Today, we're going to learn about **exclamatory sentences**.

> An exclamatory sentence expresses sudden or strong feeling. It ends with an exclamation mark.

Like a declarative sentence, an exclamatory sentence can give information, but the exclamation mark tells us that strong or sudden feelings are involved. Look at these sentences from *The Box-Car Children*, and notice the strong feelings expressed, like surprise or astonishment:

> "So you are the children who lived in the freight car!"

Exclamatory sentences can express happiness or contentment:

> "What a beautiful room this is!"

Exclamatory sentences can express any kind of sudden or strong feelings. Can you give some examples? What sentence might you exclaim if your mother were baking a cake? If you won a game? If your dog ran off with your favorite toy?

We can change each of these exclamations to statements or questions! To do this, we sometimes have to rearrange the words a little, and each declarative sentence must end in a period. Can you change the sentences above? Here are some examples of how you can do that:

"Are you the children who lived in the freight car?"

"This is a beautiful room."

Try Again
By William Hickson

Tis a lesson you should heed,
Try Again;
If at first you don't succeed,
Try again.
Then your courage should appear,
For if you will persevere,
You will conquer, never fear,
Try again.
If you would at last prevail,
Try again.
If we strive, 'tis no disgrace
Though we did not win the race;
What should we do in that case?
Try again.
If you find your task is hard.
Try again;
All that other folk can do,
Why with patience, may not you?
Only keep this rule in view,
Try again.

The Monkey and the Camel
An Aesop's Fable

At a great celebration in honor of King Lion, the Monkey was asked to dance for the company. His dancing was very clever indeed, and the animals were all highly pleased with his grace and lightness.

The praise that was showered on the Monkey made the Camel envious. He was very sure that he could dance quite as well as the Monkey, if not better, so he pushed his way into the crowd that was gathered around the Monkey and, rising on his hind legs, began to dance. But the big hulking Camel made himself very ridiculous as he kicked out his knotty legs and twisted his long clumsy neck. Besides, the animals found it hard to keep their toes from under his heavy hoofs.

At last, when one of his huge feet came within an inch of King Lion's nose, the animals were so disgusted that they set upon the Camel in a rage and drove him out into the desert.

Shortly afterward, refreshments, consisting mostly of Camel's hump and ribs, were served to the company.

Do not try to ape your betters.

Copywork

Literature

"And what am I going to do?" asked Jess, curiously.

Poetry—If You See a Tiny Fairy

And run away,

Do not stay to peek!

Exercise

Exercises can be done orally, or you can use the page in the optional workbook.

Find the adjectives in the following passage.

Here the rooms were not quite so large. They were sunny and homelike.

Find the pronouns in the following passage. Which are singular and which are plural?

"But we never could have done it without Watch. He stayed and looked after them while I was away, and he just thinks everything of Jess."

101. 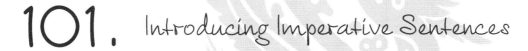 Introducing Imperative Sentences

• The Orange Fairy Book: How Ian Direach Got the Blue Falcon

A sentence begins with a capital letter and ends with a punctuation mark, and it must express a complete thought. Look at these groups of words. Which is a sentence?

Ian Direach would tell them tales of the deeds of his fathers.

On a morning.

The first group of words is a sentence because it does express a complete thought. It tells of Ian Direach and what he would do—tell them tales! The second group of words is not a sentence. It is a fragment because it does not express a complete thought. It does not tell us anything about what happened on a morning.

There are four types of sentences, and you've learned about three:

- A declarative sentence makes a statement. Its purpose is to give information, and it ends with a period.

- An interrogative sentence asks a question. It ends with a question mark.

- An exclamatory sentence expresses sudden or strong feeling. It ends with an exclamation mark.

Today, we're going to learn about the last type, **imperative sentences**. Do you know what **imperator** means in Latin? An **imperator** was a Roman general. Do you know what generals do? They give commands!

An imperative sentence gives a command or makes a request. It ends with a period.

Look at these commands, or imperative sentences, from "How Ian Direach Got the Blue Falcon":

"You shall stand with one foot on the great house and another on the castle till I come back again."

"You must first bring us the bay colt of the King of Erin."

These sentences are commands, or imperative sentences, because they give a command or make a request. They end in a period, but they do not simply give information like statements. You probably hear imperative sentences every day, such as:

Please set the table.

You should do your lessons.

Eat your dinner.

Clean your room, please.

Can you think of more?

We can change each of these commands to statements, questions, or exclamations! To do this, we sometimes have to rearrange the words a little, and each declarative sentence must end in a period. Can you change the sentences above? Here are some examples of how you can do that:

Will you set the table, please?

You should do your lessons!

You ate your dinner.

Did you clean your room?

Review

Name all the punctuation marks in the sentence below. Can you point out the contraction? Which two words made up the contraction?

"I am going away to hunt," said the king one morning.

The High Chair

By Christopher Morley

Grimly the parent matches wit and will:
Now, Weesy, three more spoons! See Tom the cat,
He'd drink it. You want to be big and fat
Like Daddy, don't you? (Careful now, don't spill!)
Yes, Daddy'll dance, and blow smoke through his nose,
But you must finish first. Come, drink it up—
(Splash!) Oh, you must keep both hands on the cup.
All gone? Now for the prunes....
　　　　And so it goes.

This is the battlefield that parents know,
Where one small splinter of old Adam's rib
Withstands an entire household offering spoons.
No use to gnash your teeth. For she will go
Radiant to bed, glossy from crown to bib
With milk and cereal and a surf of prunes.

The Wild Boar and the Fox

An Aesop's Fable

A Wild Boar was sharpening his tusks busily against the stump of a tree when a Fox happened by. Now the Fox was always looking for a chance to make fun of his neighbors. So he made a great show of looking anxiously about, as if in fear of some hidden enemy. But the Boar kept right on with his work.

"Why are you doing that?" asked the Fox at last with a grin. "There isn't any danger that I can see."

"True enough," replied the Boar, "but when danger does come, there will not be time for such work as this. My weapons will have to be ready for use then, or I shall suffer for it."

Preparedness for war is the best guarantee of peace.

Copywork

Literature

"I am going away to hunt," said the king one morning.

Maxim

Birds of a feather flock together.

Exercise

Exercises can be done orally, or you can use the page in the optional workbook.

Find the verbs in the following passage. Which are linking verbs and which are action verbs?

And in his dream a soft nose touched him, and a warm body curled up beside him, and a low voice whispered to him.

Find all of the nouns in the following passage. Which nouns are common and which are proper?

With that Ian Direach awoke and beheld Gille Mairtean the fox.

102. Narration: The Sheep and the Pig

- The Orange Fairy Book: The Fox and the Wolf

After listening to the Aesop's fable, tell the story to your instructor while she writes it down for you.

The Sheep and the Pig

An Aesop's Fable

One day a shepherd discovered a fat Pig in the meadow where his Sheep were pastured. He very quickly captured the porker, which squealed at the top of its voice the moment the Shepherd laid his hands on it. You would have thought, to hear the loud squealing, that the Pig was being cruelly hurt. But in spite of its squeals and struggles to escape, the Shepherd tucked his prize under his arm and started off to the butcher's in the market place.

The Sheep in the pasture were much astonished and amused at the Pig's behavior and followed the Shepherd and his charge to the pasture gate.

"What makes you squeal like that?" asked one of the Sheep. "The Shepherd often catches and carries off one of us. But we should feel very much ashamed to make such a terrible fuss about it like you do."

"That is all very well," replied the Pig, with a squeal and a frantic kick. "When he catches you, he is only after your wool. But he wants my bacon! Gree-ee-ee!"

It is easy to be brave when there is no danger.

Winter and Summer

By Oliver Herford

In Winter when the air is chill,
And winds are blowing loud and shrill,
All snug and warm I sit and purr,
Wrapped in my overcoat of fur.

In Summer quite the other way,
I find it very hot all day,

But Human People do not care,
For they have nice thin clothes to wear.

And does it not seem hard to you,
When all the world is like a stew,
And I am much too warm to purr,
I have to wear my Winter Fur?

Copywork

Literature

"Have you no pity for a poor mother?" asked the fox.

103.  Noun Review

- The Orange Fairy Book: The Goldsmith's Fortune

A noun is the name of a person, place, thing, or idea.

Today we're going to review nouns. Nouns are naming words. Everything has a name, and all of those names are nouns.

- Nouns name people.

Mother and **father**, **sister** and **brother**, **doctor** and **librarian**—all of these words name people, so they are all nouns. All of these nouns are **common nouns**. There are many mothers, fathers, sisters, brothers, doctors, and librarians in the world. But each individual person has their own special, proper name as well. In your literature reading this year, you've heard stories about Peter Rabbit and Mr. MacGregor, Mowgli and Bagheera. You've read about brothers and sisters— Cyril, Anthea, Robert, Jane, and Lamb from *Five Children and It* and Henry, Jess, Violet, and Benny from *The Box-Car Children*. All of these are proper nouns because they name specific characters in these stories.

- Nouns name places.

Zoo, **city**, **state**, and **ocean** are all nouns because they name places. These are common nouns, but we can also talk about the Pana'ewa Rainforest Zoo, Oklahoma City, Texas, and the Pacific Ocean. These are proper nouns naming specific places.

- Nouns name things.

Candy, snack, book, and car are all nouns because they name things. These are all common nouns. Can we have names for things which are proper nouns? Yes, we can! Do you have a favorite candy? My favorite is Reese's Peanut Butter Cups. That's the special, proper name for the kind of candy. The names of books are proper, too, like *The Orange Fairy Book*.

- Nouns name ideas.

Peace, freedom, and happiness are all nouns because they name ideas.

The Gardener

By Robert Louis Stevenson

The gardener does not love to talk.
He makes me keep the gravel walk;
And when he puts his tools away,
He locks the door and takes the key.

Away behind the currant row,
Where no one else but cook may go,
Far in the plots, I see him dig,
Old and serious, brown and big.

He digs the flowers, green, red, and blue,
Nor wishes to be spoken to.
He digs the flowers and cuts the hay,
And never seems to want to play.

Silly gardener! summer goes,
And winter comes with pinching toes,
When in the garden bare and brown
You must lay your barrow down.

Well now, and while the summer stays,
To profit by these garden days
O how much wiser you would be
To play at Indian wars with me!

The Wolf and the Shepherd

An Aesop's Fable

A Wolf had been prowling around a flock of Sheep for a long time, and the Shepherd watched very anxiously to prevent him from carrying off a Lamb. But the Wolf did not try to do any harm. Instead he seemed to be helping the Shepherd take care of the Sheep. At last the Shepherd got so used to seeing the Wolf about that he forgot how wicked he could be.

One day he even went so far as to leave his flock in the Wolf's care while he went on an errand. But when he came back and saw how many of the flock had been killed and carried off, he knew how foolish he was to trust a Wolf.

Once a wolf, always a wolf.

Copywork

Literature

"You sold your dead wife?" cried the people.

Poetry—If You See a Tiny Fairy

Do not tell

Exercise

Exercises can be done orally, or you can use the page in the optional workbook.

Find the verbs in the following passage. Which are linking verbs and which are action verbs?

> Every evening the goldsmith walked across to the cowherd's house and said, "Come. Let's go out for a walk!"

Find all of the nouns in the following passage. Which nouns are common and which are proper?

> "Why, down in that place in the river where you threw me in, I found meadows, and trees, and fine pastures, and buffalo, and all kinds of cattle."

104. *Pronoun Review*

- The King of the Golden River by John Ruskin, Chapter 1

A pronoun is a word used in the place of a noun.

We use pronouns to simplify our speech and writing. Consider this sentence:

<u>Gluck</u> did not, of course, agree particularly well with <u>Gluck's</u> brothers, or, rather, <u>Gluck's brothers</u> did not agree with <u>Gluck</u>.

That's rather a lot to say! Now consider the same sentence with the pronouns back in the sentence:

<u>He</u> did not, of course, agree particularly well with <u>his</u> brothers, or, rather, <u>they</u> did not agree with <u>him</u>.

We use different pronouns depending on whom or what we are talking about. This is automatic to you because you've been hearing these pronouns since you were a baby!

Remember that singular means only one, and plural means more than one.

- First person pronouns are used when you talk about yourself. The first person singular pronouns are I, me, my, mine. The first person plural pronouns are we, us, our, ours.

- Second person pronouns are used for the person you are talking to. The second person pronouns are you, your, yours. These pronouns are both singular and plural!

- Third person pronouns are used for the person or things that you are talking about. The third person singular pronouns are he, him, his, she, her, hers, it, its. The third person plural pronouns are they, them, their, theirs.

May Day

By Sara Teasdale

A delicate fabric of bird song
    Floats in the air,
The smell of wet wild earth
    Is everywhere.

Red small leaves of the maple
    Are clenched like a hand,
Like girls at their first communion
    The pear trees stand.

Oh I must pass nothing by
    Without loving it much,
The raindrop try with my lips,
    The grass with my touch;

For how can I be sure
    I shall see again
The world on the first of May
    Shining after the rain?

The Peacock and the Crane

An Aesop's Fable

    A Peacock, puffed up with vanity, met a Crane one day and, to impress him, spread his gorgeous tail in the Sun.

    "Look," he said. "What have you to compare with this? I am dressed in all the glory of the rainbow while your feathers are gray as dust!"

    The Crane spread his broad wings and flew up toward the sun.

    "Follow me if you can," he said. But the Peacock stood where he was among the birds of the barnyard while the Crane soared in freedom far up into the blue sky.

    The useful is of much more importance and value than the ornamental.

Copywork

Literature

    Just as he spoke, there came a double knock at the house door.

Maxim

    To be good is the mother of to do good.

Exercise

Exercises can be done orally, or you can use the page in the optional workbook.

Find the adjectives in the following passage.

He turned and turned, and the roast got nice and brown.

Find the pronouns in the following passage. Which are singular and which are plural?

He did not, of course, agree particularly well with his brothers, or, rather, they did not agree with him.

Visit to the Nursery by Jean-Honore Fragonard

Picture Study

1. Read the title and the name of the artist. Study the picture for several minutes, then put the picture away.

2. Describe the picture.

3. Look at the picture again. Do you notice any details that you missed before? What do you like or dislike about this painting? Does it remind you of anything?

105. Verb Review; Picture Study: Visit to the Nursery

- The King of the Golden River, Chapter 2

A verb is a word that shows action or state of being.

A verb is a word that shows action. Can you **waddle** like a duck? Can you **jump** really high? Can you **draw** a picture? All of the bold words are action verbs. They tell us what you do. If you can do something, it is an action verb.

Usually, we can **observe** action verbs. If you waddle or jump or draw, I can see you doing those things. There are some action verbs that we can't observe. We can't see it when someone **thinks**, or when someone **knows** something, or when someone **dreams**. These are all still action verbs. We can do these things, but others can't observe the action.

The state of being verbs are
am, are, is, was, were, be, being, been.

The linking verbs are
am, are, is, was, were, be, being, been, become, seem.

Most of the linking verbs are also state of being verbs. Linking means to connect or join. Linking verbs connect a noun or a pronoun with more information about the person, place, thing, or idea.

State of being verbs only show that someone or something exists. They don't tell us anything else about the noun or pronoun. But we can also use them as linking verbs to say something interesting about the noun or pronoun. Look at these sentences from *The King of the Golden River*. Which words are linked by the linking verbs?

The inheritance of the three brothers <u>was</u> a desert.

They <u>were</u> rather coarse.

"Goldsmithing <u>is</u> a good knave's trade."

The Sunshine

By Mary Howitt

I love the sunshine everywhere
In wood and field, and glen;
I love it in the busy haunts
Of town-imprisoned men.

I love it when it streameth in
The humble cottage door,
And casts the chequered casement-shade
Upon the red brick floor.

I love it where the children lie
Deep in the clovery grass,
To watch among the twining roots
The gold-green beetles pass.

How beautiful, where dragon-flies
Are wondrous to behold,
With rainbow wings of gauzy pearl,
And bodies blue and gold!

How beautiful on harvest-slopes
To see the sunshine lie;
Or on the paler reaped fields
Where yellow shocks stand high!

Oh! yes; I love the sunshine!
Like kindness or like mirth,
Upon a human countenance
Is sunshine on the earth!

Upon the earth; upon the sea;
And through the crystal air,
On piled up clouds; the gracious sun;
Is glorious everywhere.

Copywork

Literature

"Bless me, what's that?" exclaimed Gluck, jumping up.

Exercise

Exercises can be done orally, or you can use the page in the optional workbook.

Find the verbs in the following passage. Which are linking verbs and which are action verbs?

> The thought was agreed to be a very good one; they hired a furnace and turned goldsmiths.

Find all of the nouns in the following passage. Which nouns are common and which are proper?

> "Suppose we turn goldsmiths," said Schwartz to Hans as they entered the large city.

106. Adjective Review

• The King of the Golden River, Chapter 3

An adjective is a word that modifies a noun or a pronoun.

Cat is a noun. If someone told you that she saw a cat, you might want to know more about the cat. Was its hair long or short? What color was it? Was it friendly? Many adjectives tell us more about nouns and pronouns by describing them.

Adjectives can also modify nouns by telling us how many or how much, either with numbers or with words like **much** or **few**.

Look at these sentences from *The King of the Golden River*. The underlined words are adjectives.

> Next morning he got up before the sun rose, put the <u>holy</u> water into a <u>strong</u> flask, and <u>two</u> bottles and <u>some</u> meat in a basket, slung them over his back, took his <u>alpine</u> staff in his hand, and set off for the mountains.

Holy describes the water that Hans steals from the church! He places **two** bottles and **some** meat in a basket; **two** and **some** both tell us how much. His staff is an **alpine** staff, which means that it is made from a tree that was grown in the mountains.

Nouns only name a person, place, thing, or idea. Adjectives describe or modify the person, place, thing, or idea. They help us to picture exactly how the scene appeared.

Afternoon on a Hill

By Edna St. Vincent Millay

I will be the gladdest thing
Under the sun!
I will touch a hundred flowers
And not pick one.

I will look at cliffs and clouds
With quiet eyes,

Watch the wind bow down the grass,
And the grass rise.

And when lights begin to show
Up from the town,
I will mark which must be mine,
And then start down!

The Wolf and His Shadow

An Aesop's Fable

A Wolf left his lair one evening in fine spirits and an excellent appetite. As he ran, the setting sun cast his shadow far out on the ground, and it looked as if the wolf were a hundred times bigger than he really was.

"Why," exclaimed the Wolf proudly, "see how big I am! Fancy me running away from a puny Lion! I'll show him who is fit to be king, he or I."

Just then an immense shadow blotted him out entirely, and the next instant a Lion struck him down with a single blow.

Do not let your fancy make you forget realities.

Copywork

Literature

"Water!" he stretched his arms to Hans and cried feebly.

Poetry—If You See a Tiny Fairy

Or you'll break a fairy spell.

Exercise

Exercises can be done orally, or you can use the page in the optional workbook.

Find the adjectives in the following passage.

His way now lay straight up a ridge of bare red rocks.

Find the pronouns in the following passage. Which are singular and which are plural?

"Three drops are enough," he thought. "I may, at least, cool my lips with it."

107. *Review*

• The King of the Golden River, Chapter 4

It's time for another review!

Can you name the vowels? When is **y** a vowel?

The vowels are **a**, **e**, **i**, **o**, **u**, and sometimes **y**. **Y** is a vowel when it sounds like a vowel. When it says /y/, it's acting as a consonant.

Can you name the days of the week?

The days of the week are Sunday, Monday, Tuesday, Wednesday, Thursday, Friday, and Saturday. What day of the week is it today?

Can you name the four seasons?

The four seasons are winter, spring, summer, and fall.

Can you name the months of the year?

The months of the year are January, February, March, April, May, June, July, August, September, October, November, and December.

A June Day

By Sara Teasdale

I heard a red-winged black-bird singing
Down where the river sleeps in the reeds;
That was morning, and at noontime
A humming-bird flashed on the jewel-weeds;
Clouds blew up, and in the evening,
A yellow sunset struck through the rain,
Then blue night, and the day was ended
That never will come again.

The Frogs Who Wished for a King

An Aesop's Fable

The Frogs were tired of governing themselves. They had so much freedom that it had spoiled them, and they did nothing but sit around croaking in a bored manner and wishing for a government that could entertain them with the pomp and display of royalty and rule them in a way to make them know they were being ruled. No milk and water government for them, they declared. So they sent a petition to Jupiter asking for a king.

Jupiter saw what simple and foolish creatures they were, but to keep them quiet and make them think they had a king, he threw down a huge log, which fell into the water with a great splash. The Frogs hid themselves among the reeds and grasses, thinking the new king to be some fearful giant. But they soon discovered how tame and peaceable King Log was. In a short time the younger Frogs were using him for a diving platform while the older Frogs made him a meeting place where they complained loudly to Jupiter about the government.

To teach the Frogs a lesson, the ruler of the gods now sent a Crane to be king of Frogland. The Crane proved to be a very different sort of king from old King Log. He gobbled up the poor Frogs right, and left and they soon saw what fools they had been. In mournful croaks, they begged Jupiter to take away the cruel tyrant before they should all be destroyed.

"How now!" cried Jupiter "Are you not yet content? You have what you asked for, and so you have only yourselves to blame for your misfortunes."

Be sure you can better your condition before you seek to change.

Copywork

Literature

> But the thirst for gold prevailed over his fear, and he rushed on.

Maxim

> Good things come to those who wait.

Exercise

Exercises can be done orally, or you can use the page in the optional workbook.

Find the verbs in the following passage. Which are linking verbs and which are action verbs?

> But Gluck was very sorry and cried all night.

Find all of the nouns in the following passage. Which nouns are common and which are proper?

> And when Schwartz stood by the brink of the Golden River, its waves were black like thunder clouds, but their foam was like fire.

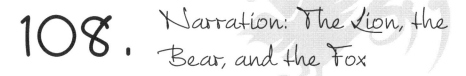

108. Narration: The Lion, the Bear, and the Fox

- The King of the Golden River, Chapter 5

After listening to the Aesop's fable, tell the story to your instructor while she writes it down for you.

The Lion, the Bear, and the Fox

An Aesop's Fable

Just as a great Bear rushed to seize a stray kid, a Lion leaped from another direction upon the same prey. The two fought furiously for the prize until they had received so many wounds that both sank down unable to continue the battle.

Just then a Fox dashed up and, seizing the kid, made off with it as fast as he could go while the Lion and the Bear looked on in helpless rage.

"How much better it would have been," they said, "to have shared in a friendly spirit."

Those who have all the toil do not always get the profit.

At the Sea Side

By Robert Louis Stevenson

When I was down beside the sea
A wooden spade they gave to me
   To dig the sandy shore.

My holes were empty like a cup.
In every hole the sea came up,
   Till it could come no more.

Copywork

Literature

"Oh dear me!" said Gluck. "Have you really been so cruel?"

Made in the USA
Columbia, SC
21 February 2023